DYNAMIC COMMUNITY LIBRARY

Creative, Practical,
and Inexpensive
Ideas for the Director

BETH WHEELER FOX

AMERICAN LIBRARY ASSOCIATION

Chicago and London 1988

"It Can Do Anything," page 6, reprinted by permission from the *Westlake* (Texas) *Picayune*

Viola Swamp, page 69, from *Miss Nelson Is Missing* by Harry Allard and James Marshall. Copyright © 1977 by Harry Allard. Copyright © 1977 by James Marshall. Reprinted by permission of Houghton Mifflin Company.

Letter to teachers, page 84, courtesy of Victoria (Texas) Public Library

Design for the Samuel Wentworth Library bookmark, page 86, by "Bill" Congdon of Sandwich, New Hampshire

Book bag logo, page 90, artwork by Robert Cline

Type style comparison guide, page 98, reproduced with permission of Graphic Products Corporation, Rolling Meadows, IL 60008. Copyright 1986.

Univers typesets, page 99, courtesy of Prestype, Inc.

Bookmark, page 100, courtesy of Waco–McLennan County (Texas) Library

Clip art, page 101, from *Library Clip Art* (ALA, 1983).

Cover and text designed by Charles Bozett

Composed in Caslon 540 and Gill Sans Bold
by Consolidated Services, Inc.

Printed on 50-pound Glatfelter, a pH-neutral
stock, and bound in 10-point Carolina
cover stock by Malloy Lithographing, Inc.

∞

Library of Congress Cataloging-in-Publication Data

Fox, Beth Wheeler.
    The dynamic community library : creative, practical, and
inexpensive ideas for the director / Beth Wheeler Fox.
       p.   cm.
    Bibliography: p.
    Includes index.
    ISBN: 0-8389-0496-3
    1. Libraries and community.   2. Small libraries—Administration.
3. Public libraries—Administration.   4. Public relations— Libraries.
I. Title.
Z716.4.F69 1988
021.2—dc19   88-10057
                                                  CIP

CONTENTS

ODE TO THE SMALL COMMUNITY LIBRARIAN

Like Bartholomew Cubbins of Dr. Seuss fame, the community librarian wears 500 hats. The smaller the staff, the more extensive the responsibilities: cataloger, publicist, fundraiser, researcher, policymaker, reader's advisor—the list goes on and on. In the very small community, the librarian probably also empties the wastebasket. The acronym OMB (One Man Band) delightfully sums up the diversity of duties.

My duties as librarian go far beyond what I learned in library school eons ago. As an administrator, I supervise and train from sixty to seventy volunteers a week, coordinate library programs like the summer reading program, attend a minimum of three meetings a week (library board, Friends organization, fundraising, publicity, etc.), make budget decisions, and maintain files for all aspects of the library. I select and order all books, deal with interlibrary loan requests, answer reference questions, answer twenty to thirty phone calls a day, and try to maintain a pleasant atmosphere. I am certainly not unique. Across the United States, librarians in small libraries are budgeting, coordinating, programming, and juggling just as effectively. Because we love the daily challenge and the active involvement with our communities, most of us continue our work in spite of low pay and marginal community support. As Diane Gordon Kadanoff said, "I think it is time that we received some recognition and respect for the terrific job we do. We are the most overlooked and underrated segment of the library profession and I want to speak out for all of us who work in the small public library. You should know that you are the backbone of the profession. Be proud of the excellent job you do and continue to enjoy your work."[1]

THE DYNAMIC COMMUNITY LIBRARY is a manual/workbook written for the library director and covering the many aspects of administration with emphasis on the library's relationship to the community. The day-to-day mechanics of running a library is not covered. The book focuses on the problems typical of small libraries. While many concerns and solutions are applicable to mid-size, branch, or even school libraries, the heart of the book is directed at the community library. The term *small library* or *community library* has been used interchangeably to refer to public libraries serving a population of less than 25,000 people.

Practical, inexpensive approaches to revitalize, to reawaken, to literally dust off the community library are explored in the following chapters. Emphasis is placed on concrete ideas that even libraries with small budgets can implement. Specific guidelines are given whenever possible.

Small libraries are often defined in terms of isolation. Physical distance as well as organizational isolation present major hurdles for the small community library. The 1980 census showed a striking development, one that the nation had not experienced in the last one hundred years: the population grew faster outside our metropolitan areas than inside them. While suburbs were still the fastest-growing areas, the growth of the rural population in our small villages and in the open countryside was the greatest since the 1870s.

Statistics show that of the 8,600 public libraries in the United States, 78 percent serve populations of less than 25,000.[2] In a 1983 survey of 1,100 rural libraries, 80 percent of their funding came from local governments. The mean budget was $82,041, although 12 percent received less than $5,000. Over 55.7 percent of the rural librarians did not have a master's degree.[3] The goal of national library standards is certainly desirable, yet the reality in community libraries is often quite different.

The staff, frequently consisting of one underpaid and overworked librarian, is overwhelmed by demands of daily operation. He or she rarely has the chance to consider alternate approaches to administration, funding, involvement of new people, or even basic library services. In most cases the beleaguered librarian wants concise, relevant words of advice, not a four-page bibliography on the community power structure.

Clearly, funding problems, availability of equipment, and training and size of staff limit the potential of the community library. Careful review of priorities is necessary to maximize use of time and money. Time management specialists would be overwhelmed by the fractured nature of the average community library. Nevertheless, "planning what should be attempted for the coming year, the coming month and the day ahead *puts the librarian in control of library development.*"[4]

All of us fall into the pit of continuing a procedure because it has always been done that way. Learn to critique every step of every process. Be sure that the time and energy expended are worthwhile. Not only is it necessary

The librarian in control

to justify a procedure, but it is also necessary to know where it falls as a priority.

Identification and use of *all* available resources enable the librarian to achieve goals more effectively. The amount of time saved by using volunteers allows the staff to do other chores. The money saved when equipment is donated can be spent in other areas.

Much has been written about the day-to-day mechanics of operating a library. Far less information is available about creating and maintaining community awareness of the library's services and needs. Most librarians in small communities are forced to deal with marginal funding, low circulation, and community apathy, yet these critical issues are rarely addressed during professional training or in library literature.

Although seldom mentioned in the job description, responsibility for community involvement will almost assuredly fall on the administration, the director, the librarian—otherwise known as *you*. Board members, volunteers, library users, and people in the community can create and carry out ideas and programs, but *you* will need to be the overall coordinator and chief cheerleader.

Active involvement by a large portion of the community is critical to future funding and usage, and in some cases even to the library's survival. The same principles of involvement exist in all communities. The following pages will help focus attention on the various components of a successful program to revitalize the community library—image, resources, services, publicity, funding, and planning.

An outreaching, active, dynamic library will have a new role in the community, and this in turn will provide a veritable cornucopia of benefits for the library and for the community.

It would be impossible to adequately thank the volunteers and board members of the Westbank Community Library, who supplied an endless variety of problems and solutions as well as laughter and enthusiasm that in turn provided the author with the practical experience to write this book. I am indebted to Anne Woods, who supplied the whimsical pen-and-ink illustrations. Bob Gaines, who always shared his expertise with humor and warmth, deserves special thanks, as does Anne Ramos, who located source material.

Most of all I wish to extend my heartfelt appreciation to Marjorie Woodberry Wheeler, who researched, read, critiqued, and supplied encouragement throughout the entire process.

Notes

1. Diane Gordon Kadanoff, "Small Libraries—No Small Job!" *Library Journal* 111 (March 1, 1986): 72–73.

2. Thomas J. Hennen, Jr., "Attacking the Myths of Small Libraries," *American Libraries*, 17 (December 1986): 830–34.

3. John W. Head, "The National Rural Library Reference Survey," *RQ*, 23 (Spring 1984): 316–21.

4. Joseph L. Wheeler and Herbert Goldhor, *Practical Administration of Public Libraries* (New York: Harper and Row, 1962), 436.

Chapter 1

YOUR RESERVE TEAM

Many libraries suffer from poor funding, low usage, and/or community apathy. There is a unique opportunity in small communities to dust off the library, to recreate interest, to involve new people, and to secure effective funding. It is a tremendous advantage that the community *is* small, because the librarian already knows much about potential resources. One quote that sums up the problem is "the essentially passive library cannot be allowed to continue undisturbed in its inertia."[1]

In all communities, no matter how small, resources abound. The great secret is to identify and then effectively use these various sources. Resources can be people, government agencies, other libraries, community groups, schools, and businesses. Resources include your volunteers, your advisory council, your Friends, and your library board. By involving large numbers of people, you create the strongest public relations campaign that can be made—people talking to people about their commitment to the library. Not only is awareness created, but a large number of people will be available to assist with funding concerns. Everyone involved with the library becomes a goodwill ambassador as well as being a taxpayer.

Label a file folder "Resources," and fill it with stray pieces of paper that identify the manager of Sears, a local beer distributor, a former librarian, a state lobbyist, the owner of a large ranch, a belly dancer, a former insurance claims adjuster, etc. By keeping the system simple, you will not be overwhelmed with update and maintenance concerns, yet you will have a ready source of valuable names. As the year progresses, you will be amazed at the variety of activities in which the library is involved and the subsequent value of the resource file.

Realities of a Volunteer Program

The heart of community involvement starts with the volunteers. The Westbank Community Library now has between sixty and seventy work-

1

ers who volunteer every week. Many librarians would topple into insanity with that sort of activity, yet there are very definite advantages to a strong volunteer program.

The first is that volunteers are obviously a source of labor. Because many libraries operate with one paid staff member, enormous amounts of work would never get done without volunteers. Even though the librarian's productive time will be greatly reduced by questions and interruptions, the volunteers produce much more work than one person. In three years, the Westbank Community Library has grown from fifty boxes of books to a dynamic community library of 18,000 books with an annual circulation of 40,000 volumes. Obviously this could not have been done with only one staff member.

Volunteers come in every size, shape, and age. Background and skills vary tremendously. The secret of successfully working with volunteers is to assume that each person has something special to offer and then to take the time and trouble to find out what it is.

Volunteers come in all shapes and forms

Volunteers can have a fulltime job and work at the library in the evenings or on Saturdays. Retired people often want a chance to contribute something to their community. Volunteers can be teenagers who belong to a service club. The list is truly endless, if *you* want it to be.

All volunteers will have certain traits in common. They will love libraries and think the library is an important part of their community. They will want to be continually busy while they volunteer their valuable time. They will think that the time they give is "professional" time, even if they are gluing in book pockets. They must feel good about their work and have pride in the library. They will probably want to socialize with people who use the library and with each other.

Socializing is not only inevitable but also desirable—after all, this is a community library. Pay attention to the personalities of your volunteers. If at all possible have them work with someone they will enjoy. In one instance, two retired couples share the work of the four o'clock to six o'clock shift. There is absolutely no need for four volunteers at this time, but they enjoy their work and *never* miss an evening.

A very small community of 850 people has eight women who have worked at the library for years. All eight work on the same morning at a long table where they process books and talk about everything under the sun. If the idea of volunteers gives you a headache, consider having groups of volunteers work together as a solution. The volunteers will often be able to answer each other's questions as well as to socialize with one another rather than with you.

TRAINING

While a volunteer's time may be "free," it has value to the person who volunteers! All volunteers should be trained to work at the circulation desk as well as at several other ongoing jobs that can be done in two- or three-hour increments. Volunteers will not need to ask for work and for the most part will be able to do their work without any supervision. Always have work to keep both scheduled and unscheduled volunteers busy. You should be able to think of jobs to keep a small army busy for the next week. For example, processing can be broken into many small increments. A different volunteer can perform each of the following steps.

> Sort donated books to keep or to put in the book sale; the librarian then checks the pre-sorted selection.
> Check the card catalog to see if titles are already held.
> List Library of Congress numbers to order preprinted catalog cards.
> Assemble card sets, pockets, and labels, and put with books.
> Check cards for accuracy; price books.
> Attach labels to spines.
> Accession books.
> Stamp books with property stamp.
> Cover books with plastic jacket or contact paper.
> Check entire book for completion and pull card sets.
> Sort card sets for shelflist, etc.
> File cards on the rod.
> Drop cards into the catalog.

Please note that the librarian was involved at only one stage of the process.

PROBLEMS

Obviously there will be problems. These seem to fall into three categories. One problem may be the volunteer does not like the job he or she is doing. This is easily remedied. Amazingly, if you acknowledge the hideousness of a job, volunteers will almost always tackle it with a smile. Sentences you might use include: "Have I got a fabulous job for you!" "You're going to love this," or "This is a filthy job and I knew you would volunteer anyway." The only time a volunteer refused a job was when she was asked to take down the flocked Christmas tree for the second year in a row. *Always* tell people to be sure to tell you if they hate their job or if they cannot stand to do it anymore today. After all, you have lots of other job opportunities.

The second problem is that the volunteer is willing to do the job, but the work is unsatisfactory. This is far easier to correct in the initial stage than later on. Monitor the work closely the first few times. If he or she does not listen to your words of wisdom, try another task. Keep changing tasks until you are satisfied that the volunteer will do the work well. If all else fails, assign a task whose outcome will not reflect on the library. Possibilities are filing on the rod (where someone else checks the work) or organizing the books in the book sale.

The third problem arises because no one has the time or inclination to train or oversee the volunteer. This neglect can cause problems with the quality of work and can anger the volunteer, who has received a clear message that his or her work is unimportant. A volunteer coordinator can solve the problem, *if* you can find a volunteer coordinator. Another solution is to have experienced volunteers train new recruits.

Occasionally you will have a serious problem. You can fall back on basic management practices to find solutions. *You* are in charge of the library and must solve the problem. Sometimes volunteers may tell you how to do your job. This will rarely happen if, as administrator, you resolve problems and make decisions in a positive and firm manner. You have to let people know that you are the final authority.

After volunteers work for a time, their responsibilities should be increased. Take maximum advantage of their abilities. Examples of greater responsibilities would be writing all newspaper articles, coordinating the summer reading program, scheduling volunteers, training new recruits, compiling annual statistics (oh, heavenly), or even (dare it be said) cataloging fiction books for which cards could not be purchased.

If you have great difficulty thinking of small jobs, think of mammoth, ongoing ones. Then train someone to do it. We had failed to put LC or ISBN numbers on all our shelflist cards, so a volunteer was given this seemingly endless job. Do you want to move all your holiday books to one Dewey number? Train someone to pull the shelflist card and the catalog cards, find the book, white out the numbers, change the label, retype the cards, and finally refile the cards. This job alone can eat up a librarian's entire life.

Many library jobs are repetitious and thus are ideal for training volunteers. The purpose is to get the work done in an orderly fashion. At first, choose jobs that do not need to be completed immediately. As you build a core of volunteers, structure the work so that large tasks can be done in a timely fashion by a number of different people.

KEEPING VOLUNTEERS

What keeps a volunteer volunteering? After all, a great deal of energy has gone into recruiting and training each person. Volunteers return week after week for two reasons. One is that they enjoy themselves. Many people are very lonely, and the time they spend in the library is a chance to meet neighbors and visit with people they enjoy. The second reason is the pride that they have in their work and therefore in their library. For some, this work may be the only area of their life about which they feel good. Pride in "their library" becomes a positive aspect of the library's image within the community.

At the Westbank Community Library, the volunteers tease the librarian about her obsession with keeping labels at the same height and property stamps straight, but they are also very aware of how things look in other libraries. Comments heard after visits to other libraries: "The displays were a mess." "The signs looked like they had been made in 1950." "No one even said hello to me." Pride is a very subtle attitude and is made up of hundreds of small components.

RECRUITMENT

The most readily available source of volunteers is the people who use the library. Sounds too simple, doesn't it? Try asking longtime borrowers if they would like to work with you for a few hours a week. Even if they will not or cannot, they will be flattered that you asked. You might say, "We'd love to have you volunteer here. You probably know as much about the collection as I do." Frequently people will say that they cannot volunteer now, but that they would like to volunteer when their husband is out of the hospital or when their young child starts school.

Be sure to express your pleasure if they say yes! Have you ever offered to do a job and had the other person say, "Well . . . I'll see"? A lukewarm response is discouraging. As soon as someone offers or is recruited to volunteer, ask if he or she prefers morning, afternoon, or evening hours. Point out that most volunteers work three-hour shifts but that you are flexible. Encourage the person to commit to a specific time on a weekly basis and then follow up with an enthusiastic phone call to reinforce the commitment.

Many potential recruits think that they have to be a librarian to work in a library. Do not roll your eyes if they say that they love to read and have always wanted to work in a library. Diplomatically smile and say that they will have first option on all the new books. Point out that you have jobs for everyone and that you offer on-the-job training. People are often threatened by new situations. Some volunteers laughingly tell how terrified they were the first day they worked: "I didn't sleep the night before." "I practiced my typing all week." *Making very sure the person feels pleased about his or her work is an important part of your job.*

'It' can do anything

"It" has 60 heads, 120 arms, ready smiles and a willingness to help. It can sort, cross reference, stamp, catalog, mend, shelve and check books out and in and assess late fines. It can order, assemble and file catalog cards. It can collate, type, answer phones, enter information in the computer and answer reference questions. It can plan a party for the Library opening, and another for the end of the Summer Reading Program.

It can blow up balloons, perform magic tricks for kids, bake cookies and clean the coffee pot. It can calligraph signs, build a bulletin board and cleverly decorate it, do finger plays, sing songs and tell stories. It can give speeches, plan art show benefits and galas, design book bags and letterheads and write computer programs. It can move 50 tons of books, set up used book sales, assemble shelves and re-arrange furniture.

But, best of all "It" makes the Library a warm, friendly place that opens it's arms wide to the whole community, ready to be of service as a community library.

This "It" is the army of some 60 volunteers who have willingly donated over 10,000 hours to make the Westbank Community Library truly a community venture.

(Want to enlist in this "army"? Aunt Beth wants YOU! The volunteer corps needs more recruits, so call the Library at 327-3045 to join.)

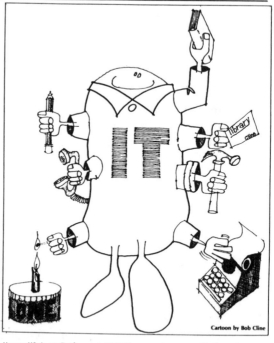

Cartoon by Bob Cline

Traffic
"What the Westbank needs is more library traffic and less Bee Cave Road traffic."
—**Cactus Pryor**

Big Ideas
"A library is such a small thing to hold so many big ideas. Congratulations to the Westbank Community Library on its first anniversary."
—**Ann Richards**

Fig. 1. Publicize your volunteer program

A volunteer who enjoys working in the library is the most effective recruiting source you have. He or she will tell friends, neighbors, and family about volunteering. No publicity campaign in the world will prove as effective.

All newspaper articles should include at least one sentence about library volunteers. (See figure 1.) Potential articles that recruit volunteers might include:

> articles highlighting an individual or group of volunteers
> humorous articles (incredible job opportunities, salary doubled every other week, choose your own hours)

articles about getting to know your neighbors through volunteering
articles asking newcomers to the community to volunteer
articles about couples volunteering to work in the evening.

Remember the group of eight women in the small community? Contact a local church group or garden club to see if the members would like to work together in the library. Groups can be used effectively to make posters, address envelopes, and stuff flyers in newspapers.

Think of everyone as a potential volunteer and involve them if at all possible. Initial involvement may be very casual. Ask a library user to help hang a new sign or assist in unjamming the copy machine. Ask regular library borrowers if they would like to help with an inventory. People feel good about helping each other, and that philosophy should and can form the basis for your recruiting program.

APPRECIATION

Every year ask the Friends organization to organize an appreciation tea for anyone who has done anything for the library. Invite people who made one poster, who fastened down the bookdrop, or who helped inventory the library. Invite all the volunteers, all the Friends, and the Board. If there is any doubt about inviting someone, invite the person anyway. Probably no more than 25 percent of those invited will come, yet all will be honored to have been invited and pleased that their work is recognized.

At Home Volunteers

An often overlooked resource is volunteers at home. These may be people with handicaps or small children or just people who want a project to do while they watch television. They can be located through special newspaper articles, through personal contact, or by word of mouth.

It is probably a good idea to start with a small task, since you will not be able to oversee the work. Assigning a small task will give you an opportunity to correct any problems or clarify the format without a lot of waste. You will also be able to see if the worker is reliable. (Strange things will happen to work that is sent home. It is still unclear how someone lost a twenty-four inch alphabetizer.)

All catalog card production for one library was done at home, as was all typing of cards, pockets, and labels. Other ideas are phoning about overdue books, addressing materials, covering paperback books, initial alphabetizing large groups of materials, organizing and scheduling volunteers, and coordinating activities for a fundraiser.

The task should be well defined. Send written instructions as well as a finished sample. Most people will prefer a deadline, although that should be negotiable. One lady carried off a box of paperbacks to cover and returned them six months later!

The Teenage Volunteer

Does the thought of teenage volunteers fill you with horror? If so, maybe this section will convince you to reconsider. Like the usefulness of everyone else, that of teenagers will vary. An often-heard generalization is that young people are just too busy to have time to volunteer. This simply is not true. Listed below are some actual examples of work done by groups of young adult volunteers. Some of the organizations listed below needed service hours. Some were looking for a worthy project, and some were involved so that the members would broaden their knowledge of the community.

> An English class conducted a weekly storytime.
> A civics class set up and cleaned up for the annual book sale.
> A 4H club, after a recent spate of exterior vandalism, was put in charge of landscaping. The librarian decided that even if the members were not the vandals, they would put peer pressure on those who were.
> A church youth group consisting of an adult and designated teen-agers operated the library every other Saturday.
> The Kiwanettes operated a booth at the annual carnival.
> Scout troops directed traffic and were responsible for cleanup at an annual event.
> The entire honor society worked one Saturday to rearrange books and shelving.
> The senior class—for pizza and cokes—gave up their weekend to "bar code" the library.
> The band, the flag girls, and the drill team performed at various fundraisers.
> A shop class built shelving for the library.

Effective use of teenage volunteers will depend on several factors. Of primary importance will be the group sponsor or leader. Another factor will be allowing appropriate lead time. Many groups will need a definite date set well in advance in order to participate. Often groups will not meet during the summer, and scheduling will then be a problem. Finally, your attitude will have a big impact on the quality of the work and the young people's enthusiasm. Like everyone else, they need to *hear* your appreciation and to feel good about the work they have done.

Individual teenagers also make wonderful volunteers. Every summer, one community library uses between twenty-five and thirty volunteers. Most of the young people are seventh, eighth, and ninth graders. (Once they can drive, they probably will get a paying job.) The teenagers are scheduled—*one at a time*—to work three-hour shifts. No one is allowed to work all day. If two teenagers work together, they should be the same sex. (Moan.) All the teens are required to attend a one-hour workshop in which basic circulation procedures and library attitudes are discussed. It is very clearly stated that they cannot wear swimsuits while they work, nor can they eat or drink except in the back room. They need to know up front that this is a business and that their attitude will be an important factor in how the library is perceived by the community.

During the last week of school, announcements are read at the middle school and high school about volunteer work at the library. All applicants fill out an application form (figure 2), which should create more of a commitment.

Conditions of Employment:

The applicant must be 13 or older. Working shifts will be for three hours. As with any job, the employee is responsible for a regular work schedule. The librarian needs to be notified in advance of any absences. The position is on a volunteer basis. All employees will be given a letter of verified employment at the end of the summer. An introductory workshop will be held _____ or _____ .

Name _____

Address _____

Phone_____

Source of Recommendation: (other than relative)

Name _____

Phone _____

Preferred Day and Hours of Employment: (Circle one)

Monday	*10–1*	*1–4*	*4–6*
Tuesday	*10–1*	*1–4*	*4–6*
Wednesday	*10–1*	*1–4*	*4–6*
Thursday	*10–1*	*1–4*	*4–6*
Friday	*10–1*	*1–4*	
Saturday	*10–1*		

Fig. 2. Sample application form for teenage volunteer

The teenagers are responsible for the circulation desk. They check books in and out, issue library cards, write overdues, answer the phone, shelve books, and handle details of the summer reading program. To be honest, the circulation desk is so hectic in the summer that adult volunteers will avoid it at all costs.

At the end of the summer, the Friends organization always provides a swim party. It is a very casual affair that lasts about two hours. The Friends provide the pool, hotdogs, potato chips, and cold drinks. The teenagers have a wonderful time. The local paper always prints a "pool picture" that identifies the teenagers by name and recognizes their volunteer work. Letters of recommendation are sent to each teenager.

Teenagers have proved to be very hard-working, very caring, and more than willing to do all kinds of tedious jobs with enthusiasm. As adults, librarians tend to offer readers' advice cautiously to children. Teenagers, particularly boys, will bounce over to the shelves, pull off a book, say, "You'll love this," and thrust it into the waiting child's hands. Both seem very satisfied with this system.

Teens like the work *very much* as long as they are busy. They receive many compliments from people using the library, from adult volunteers, and from the staff. They thrive on having a visible responsibility for which they receive recognition. Four or five will continue to work in the evening during the school year. Many will work in the library for two or three summers. All of them will be library advocates for the rest of their lives.

Library Board

The library board supplies tremendous resources and provides a way to recognize people who have already done a great deal for the library. The board controls legal and financial decisions, ensures sound management, represents the organization, and raises money. In small libraries, board members often have assigned responsibilities, such as serving as treasurer, publicity chairman, fundraiser, or corresponding secretary. The librarian must work closely with the board in order to coordinate these important tasks.

As the board changes, additions should complement and supplement the talents of current members. Professional expertise is always desirable. Library literature generally recommends a board of seven members, although this number is frequently increased if the library is involved in a major fundraising campaign. If you are planning to build a new library, do you have a CPA, a lawyer, an architect, or a land developer on your board? People who have coordinated fundraisers and survived are invaluable.

Never assume a member of the community is not interested. At the least the person will be pleased to have been asked.

TRAITS

It should be an honor to serve on the board. The smaller the community, the more visible this position is. Potential nominees need to be aware of what the position entails. Ideally there should be a job description that details the number of hours of meetings per month, lists the subcommittees board members may serve on and, most important, identifies fundraising as part of their job. If board members do not have an assigned responsibility, they should have very strong community ties. *Many publications from nonprofit organizations state that the single most improtant characteristic of a board member is the willingness to fundraise on a one-to-one basis.*

Many myths surround traits of potential leaders. Studies consistently show, however, that leaders are rarely outwardly assertive, yet when the need arises, they tackle projects that are uncomfortable for them and persevere until the job is well done. The rest of the time, they remain inconspicuously in the background. Key traits are *initiative, problem-solving abilities, thoughtful and reflective minds, flexibility, a practical outlook, self-awareness, persistence, and enthusiasm.*[2]

BOARD DEVELOPMENT

Board development is very important if the board is to be an effective tool of the library. The board needs to change and grow. A board that founds a library often needs to cope with the day-to-day mechanics. However, as the library grows, the board needs to change its focus to long-range planning and policymaking. Interestingly, a board that is overly involved is easier to redirect than a board that is stagnant and needs to be resurrected.

Consultants and workshops dealing with board development are available. Many state library systems offer workshops on board development. Seminars sponsored by other nonprofit organizations will be relevant to a library board because all these boards must cope with fundraising, long-term planning, and policymaking.

A board member that needs to be resurrected

STANDING COMMITTEES

One vital tool in creating an effective board is the standing committee. The committees actively involve more people and allow a greater variety of information into key decisions. Knowledge of major decisions is not limited to one or two people. Typical standing committees are nominating, long-term planning, and budget committees. *The nominating committee is probably the most important committee of the board because it controls the very future of the library.* This committee is often poorly utilized.

RELATIONSHIP TO LIBRARIAN

As a librarian, you need to beware of abdicating your authority to the board when you are unsure how to deal with a given situation. *Your decision will affect all future librarians.* Some librarians have no authority over book selection or even decisions about day-to-day purchase of office supplies. This lack of authority is a direct result of a former librarian's abdicating responsibility. The time to resolve authority problems is when the librarian is hired. Unfortunately, the newly-hired librarian may not even be aware an authority problem exists.

Identification, clarification, and establishment of areas of responsibility will greatly simplify your job as well as that of the board. Lines of authority in which all parties communicate and offer mutual respect and support should be a top priority of the board and of the librarian.

Advisory Council

An advisory council uses community leaders to provide commitment, advice, and leadership for a particular goal. Advisory councils are frequently created to assist in a building campaign or with a major fundraising effort. Benefits that result are

> Greater involvement of the community
> Awareness of library needs by community leaders
> Ideas and advice from people aware of the area's needs and capabilities
> Group commitment for a major effort.

The advisory council should be selected from all areas of the community. Including persons from a variety of political affiliations, ethnic minorities, civic groups, age groups, and geographic areas should be important considerations. Consider including the superintendent of schools, the mayor, the president of the school board, the state representative, the president of the local bank, and the newspaper editor. In order to avoid a reputation of bias, the council should represent a true cross section of the community.

Leadership and meetings for the council need to be planned strategically. Busy people will be antagonized by a meeting that is without a clear structure and purpose. An advisory council plans on giving advice, so be sure that the opportunity exists. The board members need to attend meetings to *hear* the advice and to offer background information as questions arise.

The meeting agenda should be mailed in advance along with other appropriate material. The length of the meeting and the purpose should be clearly identified. Minutes of the meeting need to be distributed to all committee members if possible, but especially to those members who were unable to attend.

Friends Groups

You might expect considerable overlap in membership among the various library groups. This does not seem to be the case. Perhaps the groups appeal to different types of people. Certainly a Friends group offers many advantages to any library. Such a group can organize volunteers, manage the summer reading program, coordinate storytimes, run book sales, provide appreciation teas, bring refreshments to various events, or provide cakes for the cakewalk. An effective Friends group will be available with a ready smile and a willingness to help whenever possible.

Friends organizations are frequently formed from a core of volunteers and then gradually branch out to encompass a wide variety of people in the community. Many groups operate through an executive board that meets on a regular basis and plans various activities to promote the library. Most members are involved only on the actual day of the activity.

Philosophies vary greatly as to the purpose of Friends groups. Some communities will encourage everyone to join for one dollar a year and give out membership cards, while other areas have an ongoing group of ten or more members who meet frequently and do all the work. Other Friends groups have larger annual fees of between ten and twenty-five dollars and hold membership meetings only once a year.

One Friends organization was concerned about the members who were never contacted except at renewal time. A postcard mailed quarterly, covering recent library news, solved the problem. (See figure 14.) Some members will want to be very active, and others will only want to send in their renewal dues. Be sure there is a place for everyone within the organization.

Nothing will kill a Friends group quicker than an aura of exclusiveness. Many Friends groups founder because they become, or at least are perceived as, a closed organization, particularly at the board level. This situation can be avoided only by active solicitation of new members. Pay attention to parents actively involved with children and recruit them to be in charge of children's activities. Notice who brings delicious and attractively displayed food to a bake sale, then recruit that person to be hospitality chairperson. The library, the president of the Friends, the nominating committee, and anyone else who is handy should "brainstorm" for names of new officers whenever the need arises. *A changing, active board is also a healthy board.*

Ideally, the Friends organization is a standing committee of the board. Not only will there be clear lines of authority, but both groups can use the same nonprofit tax exemption. The Friends group will not be tempted to set policy but will clearly be a support organization. The president of each organization can either be a member or ex officio member of the other board. Effective communication will then exist between the two groups. A sample constitution and bylaws for a Friends group are included in Appendix C.

Schools

Surely schoolteachers, school boards, and the school administration are the most overlooked resources available to the library. Communication and cooperation will pay dividends beyond belief; after all, the two organizations hold many goals in common.

Send the teachers a letter at the beginning of each school year or, better yet, make a presentation at each school faculty meeting. Tell the teachers that you provide a secondary resource for the schoolchildren and that you want to work together to provide effective library service. Point out strengths in the library collection. Tell them you will purchase books to help students. Offer to put books on reserve if they notify you of major assignments ahead of time, before every book on the subject is checked out. Some teachers will not know there is a public library. Give them a bookmark with the hours and phone number as well as a flyer with any helpful information. (See figure 10.) Let them know that you would *love* to have them volunteer in the library during the summer, on the weekends, or in the evenings.

SCHOOL ASSIGNMENTS

The Victoria (Texas) Public Library provides all the teaching personnel in their area with a four-page booklet, inexpensive but attractive, that answers key questions about the library. (See figure 11.)

What is available?
Will there be enough books for my assignment?

How far in advance should I call the library about my assignment?
How long can books be checked out?
Can I check out books for my students?
Can my class tour the library?

The booklet provides effective communication between the public librarian and the schoolteachers. How many of you have cursed burdensome school assignments, yet struggled to encourage teenagers to use the public library? Diplomatic discussion with the fifth-grade teacher who requires twelve magazine articles about the Statue of Liberty will go a long way to soothe your staff and will earn you everlasting gratitude from the fifth-grade parents. Teachers will be appreciative of your concern and will in turn become vocal advocates of the community library.

FIELD TRIPS

Library field trips offer benefits for the student as well as the library. Many students have never entered the public library. If you first meet with children when they are in kindergarten, you not only can introduce them to their local library but also can send information home to their parents. Many libraries issue library cards to the children and also send home a colorful flyer.

Cooperate with the art teacher and offer wall space in the library for children's art. The children and their parents will visit the library to admire the work, and the art teacher will have a location to display the work. Teachers can offer recommendations for new books. Art teachers can letter signs, design posters, and help prepare printing layouts. The journalism teacher may help with newspaper articles, perhaps making the article-writing a class project. The computer teacher will be a valuable source of assistance if you ever purchase a computer. The list is endless.

SCHOOL LIBRARIANS

School librarians should be your strongest supporters. If they are not, it is up to *you* to do something about it. Make sure they know you—take them to lunch, attend an occasional meeting—and let the school administration know how much you appreciate their cooperation. Work to complement their collections; then be sure they know what you are doing. *Communicate.*

ADMINISTRATION

The school administrators can be equally helpful. Be sure that the superintendent of schools knows *you*. You want to be able to call him or her to

Remember to communicate!

resolve simple problems. Permission will need to be obtained from the superintendent to distribute any literature in the schools. Flyers can be sent home with all elementary school children for summer reading program registration. School librarians or individual teachers may be willing to talk about the program to the children in the last few weeks of class. The administration may let you or a board member make a brief presentation to parents at various back-to-school nights. Sometimes a district will lease land or a building to the library at a nominal cost once the importance of the community library is recognized. Some elementary schools hold an annual "run" as a fundraiser for the community library. Announcements about summer volunteers can be made at the appropriate schools. During the first year of operation of the Westbank Community Library, the school administration allowed the library to borrow 500 books over the summer. Leave a paper trail of letters of appreciation behind you. Everyone appreciates acknowledgment—even the superintendent of education.

The school administration office is often the first stop for newcomers. Many districts offer a packet of information about the community. Be sure a flyer about the library is included.

The goodwill and cooperation of the school board can also provide numerous benefits. Members of school boards have a broad understanding of their community and are generally very concerned about the quality of life in the area. The support of this board may provide valuable leverage in changing the quality of community library service.

Look upon your schools as a valuable resource. Think of creative ways to work with them to help you and to help them. A lack of communication and cooperation often exists between the local library and the schools. *You* can change this almost single-handedly. You will be amazed at the positive response from the teachers, the students, and the administration.

Community Organizations

All communities have an abundance of nonprofit or specialized organizations. These organizations can benefit the library in two ways. First, the meetings can be used to "spread the word" about library services and programs. Whenever a group of people meet, an audience has been created. Program chairpersons will be delighted to have a program provided. The librarian or a volunteer can give a brief talk on services the library offers. Take along appropriate books, issue library cards, hand out bookmarks with the library's hours and phone number, be prepared to answer questions, tell them about library concerns—communicate!

Second, the organization may be able to help the library solve a problem. Is the library looking for a new location? Is the county considering eliminating library funds? Do you need more volunteers? Do you want the group's financial support? Would you like the group to landscape the library grounds? Once again, if the request is never made, the response will never happen. Chapter 2 details the importance of organizations within the community power structure and the potential role that the library can play.

Church groups, mothers of preschoolers organizations, the PTA, the Kiwanis and Lions clubs, the Masons, the Chamber of Commerce, gardening clubs, bridge clubs, youth organizations of all kinds, business organizations (such as local realtors), and neighborhood associations exist in almost every area. There are many organizations, clubs, and associations in your community! (Remember that many also have a newsletter.)

Businesses

Several types of assistance can be provided by local businesses. Occasionally, assistance will be in the form of cash. However, donations of materials or in-kind donation of services is usually more readily obtained. With few exceptions, businesspeople must first be convinced that assistance to the library will promote their businesses or provide them with tax deductions. Businesspeople will never be persuaded of potential benefits unless they are directly approached for assistance.

Thanking a business for gift to the library almost always takes the form of community recognition. This can be achieved through newspaper articles, identification on flyers, and verbal appreciation.

Chain stores, such as grocery stores, often have a budget to spend on community activities. Ice, cheese, wine, flowers, napkins, balloons, books, and carnival prizes might be donated for the asking. More expensive items can often be purchased at a significant discount. Never assume that the library has to buy an item. The smaller the community, the more valid this idea becomes. Used office furniture—including desks, files, chairs, copy machines, and typewriters—can be obtained at no cost by creating awareness of specific needs. A wish list in the form of a newspaper article or letter to the Friends organization could identify these needs. Don't forget staplers, cutting boards, coffee maker, wastebaskets, bulletin board, and even steel shelving for the workroom.

Occasionally businesses will allow you to buy furniture at wholesale prices. In one community library, all the wood furniture was purchased through a local lumber yard at a savings of 50 percent.

Don't forget to ask local businesses for in-kind or service donations. Accounting services, legal assistance, architectural plans, printing, electrical or plumbing work, surveys, and landscaping are actual examples of donated services. The library will often pay for supplies, while the labor is donated. In reality, weekly coverage in the newspaper is an in-kind donation. Many businesses place a value on such gifts for tax purposes.

Other Libraries

Librarians provide incredible resources for other librarians. All of us readily share information with one another. Without the generous help of librarians from the state library, the state association, the local library system, and nearby public and school libraries, this book would never have been written. In fact, librarians as a group are extremely generous with their time and experience. (Some would say that we love to give advice.) Developing professional contacts and learning about other libraries will help you enrich your library.

Professional associations, state library systems, and informal networks should be utilized. Small libraries pay a nominal fee to join professional associations. Professional fees should be budgeted by the library. Annual conferences offer displays of library furniture, new books, and supplies, as well as seminars or talks on a wide variety of library issues. Meeting new people and exchanging ideas can be invaluable. One sometimes wishes that more opportunities were available to sit down with librarians from similar libraries and share concerns. One librarian said she never went to conferences with her staff or friends because that precluded meeting new people.

STATE LIBRARY SYSTEMS

Individual states often provide an umbrella organization that promotes library development for public libraries. Membership is frequently based on meeting certain criteria—a certain level of funding, a minimum number of books per capita, certain hours of operation, etc. In exchange, the state will provide a wide range of services. While these will vary from state to state, they might include interlibrary loan privileges, large print books, a 16mm film collection, assistance with collection development, and workshops for professional development. To qualify for membership may be difficult for the very small library, but the returns are enormous. Contact the appropriate person and work together to qualify your library. Even if the library cannot join the state system, chances are you will still receive valuable advice and assistance from the staff.

You should be aware that states often provide specialized library services to residents. The legislative library may provide copies of current legislation. The state genealogical library is a valuable resource for researchers. Blind or handicapped readers may borrow tapes, records, or braille books from the state library. *You need to be familiar with these resources and encourage your community to use them.*

NETWORKS

Do you ever eat lunch with a neighboring librarian or call with a question about the best supplier of catalog cards? If so, you have just created an informal network. Librarians routinely need to know how to resolve an enormous variety of questions. Quick answers are rarely available. A search through library literature would provide many answers, yet the item in shortest supply is time. Just think of the benefits of sharing all this practical information with other librarians! Networking allows us to share this type of knowledge with one another. The following is the format that works best for The Network for Very Small Libraries, which was started by the author and Penelope Duke-Williams.

FORMAT FOR NETWORK MEETINGS

Meetings are small, with no more than ten people, and each person participates. A timer is used to keep track of the time.

Each meeting focuses on a topic. This gives direction to the meeting and generates discussion. Some sample topics might include fundraising, computers, volunteers, or publicity.

Schedule quarterly, two-hour meetings. As librarians with little or no staff, it is difficult to meet more frequently or for longer periods.

Meeting locations rotate among the various libraries. In this way one has a chance to visit other libraries; it also provides the librarian a chance to "show off" his or her library.

Your Filing Cabinet

The gruesome truth is that board members expect you to be able to readily find all kinds of information about the library. You will find it very useful to make a "quick and dirty" index to board minutes for each year. Have a board member or volunteer serve as historian and keep scrapbooks of any relevant photographs and news articles. The library filing cabinet should be an extremely valuable research tool, not only for current material but also for historical information about the library.

Are your files manageable? If not, here are some suggested file headings that are probably common to most small libraries. The main heading labels (Building & Land, Finances, etc.) can be color coded. Organized files will help improve *your* image.

File Headings	*File Contents*
Building & Land	Building, layout
	Building, other libraries
	Insurance
	Lease
Finances	Bank statements (folder for each account by year)
	Budget, current
	Budget, past
	Endowment board
	Financial statement (subdivided by year)
	Investments
	IRS, background
	IRS, 941 (employment)
	IRS, 990 (annual)
	IRS, W2 & W4
	Tax exempt status
	Treasurer's report
Fundraising	Advisory Council
	Background (subdivided by year)
	Events (book sale, carnival, run for the library)
	Grant applications (subdivided by each foundation)
	Resource material
Furniture & Equipment	Computer
	Copy machine
	Furniture specifications
	Inventory
	Manuals
	Service contracts
	Typewriter
Library Operations & Materials	Annual reports
	Board (subdivided by year)
	Book selection
	Cataloging
	Correspondence (subdivided by year)

File Headings	*File Contents*
Library Operations & Materials (*cont.*)	Displays
	Donations (for books)
	Filing
	Fines & overdues
	Government Printing Office
	History
	Interlibrary loan (in progress)
	Interlibrary loan (complete)
	Periodicals
	Policies
	Postage
	State library system (membership)
	State library system (services)
Miscellaneous	American Library Association
	State library association
	Regional library system
Personnel	Friends of the Library
	Librarian
	Resources
	Staff
	Volunteers
	Volunteer, teenagers
Printing & Publicity	Ideas
	Logo
	Originals
	Publicity (subdivided by year)
Programs	Ideas
	Story hour
	Summer reading program (subdivided by year)
Retired Files	
Bills Paid	(Listed alphabetically by company; subdivided by year if necessary)
	Miscellaneous (books)
	Miscellaneous (office supplies)

Conclusion

An abundance of resources exists in every community, no matter how small. Learn to identify and involve every potential volunteer in your library. The enthusiasm of each one will attract new volunteers. Like all success stories, success ensures greater success. People will view volunteering at the library as a prestigious activity and will want to be a part of the bandwagon. Picture yourself inundated by volunteers . . . .

Notes

1. Joseph L. Wheeler and Herbert Goldhor, *Practical Administration of Public Libraries* (New York: Harper and Row, 1962), 6.

2. Bill Lareau, "How to Spot a Potential Leader," *Personal Report for the Executive* (September 17, 1985): 1–2.

Recommended Reading

Altman, Ellen. *Local Public Library Administration*. 2nd ed. Chicago: American Library Association, 1980.

Rochell, Carlton. *Wheeler and Goldhor's Practical Administration of Public Libraries*. Rev. ed. New York: Harper and Row, 1981.

Setterberg, Fred, and Kary Schulman. *Beyond Profit: The Complete Guide to Managing the Nonprofit Organization*. New York: Harper and Row, 1985.

Young, Virginia, ed. *The Library Trustee: A Practical Guidebook*. 4th ed. Chicago: American Library Association, 1988.

Chapter 2

THE CUSTOM-MADE LIBRARY

What does the library offer the community? *The library must identify whom it serves, what services are wanted, how the services will be provided, and how they will be promoted.* Clearly, in order to identify the above, some research and planning are required.

The human race, including librarians, has honorable intentions of establishing priorities. In reality we often stumble along without clear guidelines. Nowhere is this more evident than in the vast array of user services offered in the community library. The purpose of this chapter is to describe ways in which librarians can learn about the people they serve and how to evaluate both current and potential activities.

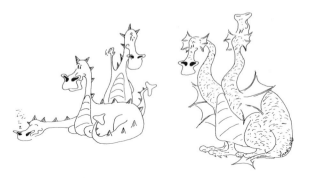

Each community is unique

Analysis of the Community

Library services begin with user needs. Awareness of the specific characteristics of your community will be necessary in order to provide the most effective service, purchase appropriate materials, improve overall recognition of the library, and demonstrate to community leaders that the library understands the community. Like fingerprints, your community is unique. Identifying specific characteristics and translating potential needs into programs and services are integral parts of maintaining a viable library. The wants or needs of the user must be identified before deciding what the library should or should not attempt.

CHARACTERISTICS

The library may be located deep in the countryside, in a small town, or in the suburbs of a large city. Accessibility to other libraries and thus other resources will be a factor. Geographic factors might include mountains, deserts, or the wide open plains. Distances to travel can be a major factor in usage. Weather conditions, such as hot summers or very cold winters, can affect services.

The ethnic makeup of the community will be a consideration. What proportion is black or Caucasian? What languages are spoken? Are there new immigrants with unique needs? Customs of various groups may have an impact.

Work ethics will vary across the country, as will local traditions. Ranchers, blue-collar workers, high-tech specialists, and working mothers have different needs and expectations. Are the people functionally illiterate, high school graduates, or college graduates? Income level and median age are other factors. Religion can be an important aspect, particularly in areas like the southern Bible belt. Politics, whether liberal or conservative, can affect the library. Does the work force commute to work or is most work done locally?

Look at population trends for the last ten years. Is the community gaining or losing population? What are the expectations for library service from new residents? Is there a large housing turnover? Is the population transient or stable?

SOURCES OF DATA

Clearly, knowledge of the community is critical to meeting needs and expectations. Whenever possible, proven census or demographic materials should be used. The U.S. census, which is updated every ten years, can be an invaluable source of demographic and economic information. For instance, population data is arranged in categories by race, sex, location, education, age, and occupation; business data is categorized by number of employees, total payroll, and products manufactured; categories for data about farms include number, acreage, and crop sales; and government data categories include revenues and expenditures, taxes, and employment. This information is available for each zip code, or for incorporated areas, although the data is more limited for towns with less than 2,500 people. Each state has a state data center, which has access to a tremendous variety of data, including U.S. census figures. Some states will charge a nominal fee to users who wish to obtain this data. The addresses for these centers are listed in the appendix of the *U.S. Census Catalog and Guide*. The first step in compiling data is to contact the appropriate state data center and request figures for your area. Some of this material is also available in *County and City Data Book* and *Census Data for Community Action*, but the state data center may have more current information from other sources as well as the resources for doing the necessary research.

Most towns with a population over 15,000 have a planning department as well as a Chamber of Commerce. Interviews with community leaders, such as town officials, business leaders, the school superintendent, the newspaper editor, and club presidents will provide valuable information. These interviews will introduce you to key leaders in the area and will demonstrate the library's commitment to planning and improvement. The purpose is to obtain as accurate a picture as possible of the library's clientele.

Many librarians already have an understanding of their community. However, the location of a new plant, the world market for oil, or spillover growth from a nearby city may have dramatically changed your community. As you develop a master plan, it will be necessary to tailor it to fit your community. *This is an ongoing process that you will constantly need to update and supplement.*

USE OF THE DATA

Typically, about 30 percent of the adult population uses the library at least once a year. Knowledge of the other 70 percent is vital in order to provide effective service. The results from a community analysis should be used to review the library's future goals and objectives, which are then translated into policies, programs, and activities, and to evaluate past performance.

Jim Fish illustrated the potential value of comparing two communities.[1] The first community had a relatively young median age of 28.3 years. Less than half of its population twenty-five years and over had a high school degree. Skilled workers made up 44.5 percent of its work force, while those employed in manufacturing made up 48.6 percent. A little over a third of the population, 38.1 percent, were of foreign stock. The second community had a median age of 33.5 years with a large elderly population. Almost 72 percent were high school graduates, and white-collar occupations accounted for 67.6 percent of the employed persons.

Even the limited statistics above provide evidence that vocational background and age factors will create very different needs for materials and programs in the two communities. The first community would probably be interested in picture books, materials on child-rearing and vocational guidance, "how-to" books, and material in languages other than English. A literacy program might provide a much needed service. Information about retirement options, travel, and investment opportunities would probably be appropriate in the second community. Informational programs would probably be well received, as would a collection of large-print books and service for the homebound.

Information collected as part of the community analysis should include both factual data and subjective impressions. *Know in advance what use will be made of each piece of information collected* and set a clear time schedule for obtaining this information. The potential information is staggering, so be sure to identify and obtain only what is most useful to you.

DATA COLLECTION

From the list below, selectively choose items to help you collect data that will influence library planning. Data that identifies populations with special needs, that revises preconceptions, that sensitizes the library to current and future trends, that targets unserved portions of the community, that suggests weak areas of the collection, or that identifies problems in using the library for the physically or mentally impaired will allow you to plan appropriate solutions. For each item ask, "What will I do differently on the basis of the information I obtain?"[2]

Geography
    Physical size of community
    Geology
    Distances
    Climate

Demographics
    Ethnic groups
    Racial groups
    Language groups
    Age categories
        Percentage under 5 years
        Percentage between 5 and 17 years
        Percentage over 65 years
    Politics
    Religion
    Education level
        Illiterate
        12 or more years of school completed
        College graduate

Economic considerations
    Income level
        Percentage below poverty level
        Average per capita income
        Median family income

Percentage of work force
    in manufacturing
    in wholesale and related services
    in government
    self-employed
    in agriculture
Unemployment rate

Housing characteristics
    Total number of households
    Average number of persons per household
    Transient versus stable population
    Average length of time in community
    Percent of commuters

Included in this data should be statistical information about the library, such as:

Total number of registered borrowers
Percentage of community which is aware of various library services
Circulation statistics
Participation in children's story hours
Audiovisual usage
Reference statistics
Use of interlibrary loan services
Use of meeting rooms
Percentage of students who have visited the library

Library Services and Programs

The average community library provides effective services and materials at nominal cost. The fact that the library has limitations is not cause for apology. A true administrator learns to say no early in his or her career. Practice this word in front of the mirror.

The collection and services offered *by* the library and *to* the community may well appeal to different individuals or groups. Justification for maintaining materials or services is as important as the initial selection. Establishment of specialized collections of magazines, pamphlets, records, and other materials should be carefully studied. The current trend recognizes that some traditional library services are offered more effectively by other public or private agencies. A separate historical museum may well be a more logical location for much of the local history collection. Avoid duplication of effort.

Practice saying "no" in front of the mirror

THE IDEAL LIBRARY

A recent survey soliciting the description of an ideal library offered the local residents a wish list for public services.

> Those interviewed want to borrow videocassettes and videocassette players . . . and rated both near the top of their lists of desired services. One in three potential patrons would borrow players; one in two, cassettes. Survey participants also identified other 'desirable' library services: convenient parking, a drive-through bookdrop, a community bulletin board, and a photocopier. They also want a knowledgeable librarian who will reserve material for them. They wish the library to be cheerful and well-lighted, and to have comfortable chairs and public rest rooms. Most agreed that a two-week loan period for books and one week for videocassettes are acceptable. They preferred that libraries be open from 4 to 8 pm on weekdays, and on Saturday mornings and afternoons. They want genealogy materials and tax forms as well as basic reference sources. Computer classes, workshops on film and other topics for adults, and children's programs were also rated high. Of lesser importance to potential library users in the survey were computer software, 8 mm or 16 mm films, microcomputers, book discussion groups, telephone books, on-line checkout and renewal from home computers, and record players, among a long list of possibilities.[3]

Every library, however, will have unique needs. Surveys produce results that can be skewed. Potential library users are *not* the same as current library users. "Wish lists" often contain some fluff. Most of us are light-years away from renewing books by home computer. Often, the addition of a new service can be staffed or funded only through elimination of another.

PROGRAMS

Program planning is limited only by your imagination, your staff, and the budget. Many programs and activities can be produced with a minimum amount of energy and money. A book full of ideas is *GO, PEP, and POP!* by Virginia Baeckler and Linda Larson. A sample page includes ideas for a lunar landscape, a geodesic dome building, elementary science experiments, and a display of sea monkeys. The authors suggest moving the essential checkout service outside and enjoying the sunshine. Other ideas include a baseball game, with the children playing the library staff, and a karate demonstration.

Successful programs and activities do not have to be elaborate or expensive. A riddle contest that changes weekly is a favorite summer activity year after year. The winner is selected in a drawing and receives an inexpensive paperback book.

Other excellent sources for ideas are *Fireworks, Brass Bands and Elephants* by Louise Condak Liebold and *Library Promotion Handbook* by Marian S. Edsall. Potential programs are discussed in detail. Programs described in Edsall's book include a discussion of the techniques of scuba diving, a demonstration of a blacksmith shoeing a pony, a talk on endangered species, an evening of Greek culture, and a taffy pull. The author points out that most library programming deals with topics of lasting interest such as

money management	gardening, landscaping
consumerism	cooking, nutrition
self-help	pet care
hobbies, crafts	nature study
health, first-aid	child care
sports	local history
retirement	job, careers
genealogy	home maintenance[4]

Located on the edge of a large city, one community library serves an affluent, well-educated community that has access to numerous programs and classes. Nevertheless, board members, volunteers, and the librarian were certain that the Great Books program and special summer storytimes would be well received. They were not, and after several attempts, the programs were eliminated. People in the community simply had a surplus of programs to choose from. *Do not compete with services already readily available.*

When selecting programs and activities, librarians should seek a balance between areas of perennial or long-term interest and those of current interest. Plan well in advance. The chart dealing with basic factors on page 40 is applicable to events, programs, or special activities. Obviously, some concerns will not be appropriate in a given situation. For some libraries, an activity will also be a fundraiser, while in others, it will be a very simple event that does not include refreshments, invitations, or even a special location.

No matter how carefully the event is planned, strange things will happen. Remember to be flexible and learn to flow with the confusion. One Friends group featured a booktalk by an author who had just published a book on wildflowers. Unfortunately, in spite of careful planning and numerous discussions with the speaker, the presentation turned out to be a ninety-minute slide show on the origin of chili peppers. The talk is now part of the library's folklore and will long be remembered with giggles by everyone who was in the audience!

PROGRAM BASICS

Committee

Identify and obtain a commitment from key people.
Agree on a rough schedule of when each area should be completed.
Establish a budget, including mailing costs, printing costs, refreshments, and rental of equipment.
Identify the purpose of the event and the expected response. Review the event after its presentation in light of these goals.

Speaker/Activity

Contact the speaker regarding topic, time, place, payment (if any), length of talk, type of audience, and physical setup.
Clarify needs for special equipment (microphone, pointer) or supplies (glitter, glue).
Obtain biographical information about the speaker for the introduction.
Send the speaker a written confirmation and invitation as well as copies of any publicity releases.
Decide who will introduce the speaker, present a small gift, and make the closing remarks.
Send a thank-you letter to the appropriate people.

Place

Obtain written approval from the person in charge of the location.
Make sure that kitchen and bathroom facilities are available if needed.
Identify person(s) responsible for setup, lockup, and cleanup.
Obtain permission to use chairs, tables, and coffee maker.

Verify that the necessary furniture is available for the expected audience.

Date and Time

Select a tentative date and time.

Verify that there are no conflicts with other major events; check the school calendar for conflicts.

Refreshments (if any)

Appoint a hospitality chair who will be responsible for contacting individuals to bring refreshments and for deciding what will be served.

Make arrangements for delivery or pickup of refreshments. Identify the person responsible for decorations (if any).

Public Relations

Decide how the public will be invited: invitations, newspaper articles, flyers, or some other method.

Appoint someone to be responsible for the format and layout of articles publicizing the event.

Establish a timeline for releasing or mailing appropriate publicity materials.

HOURS OF OPERATION

We do not tend to think of our hours of operation as a service, and yet they are. Evening and weekend hours (the most difficult time to staff the library) are frequently requested by users. Personal experience has shown that the library is poorly used during the last hour it is open—except for the final five minutes. Saturday mornings are popular but it takes several months before a core of users is established. Saturday afternoons will provide a library with high usage in some areas and almost none in others. Low use from six to eight o'clock in the evening caused one library to close at six Monday through Thursday. The typical worker will probably have no opportunity to use the library except during evening or weekend hours. Remember that every time library hours are changed, extensive publicity will be needed. Nothing irritates library patrons as much as arriving at the library at an hour when it used to be open and finding it closed.

SPECIAL AUDIENCES

Targeting special populations can prove effective. Recently, the Queens Borough Public Library initiated a program to raise awareness of its

Fotonovela—Reading Is Power

services in the Hispanic community. Under the banner "Say 'Si' to Your Library," the effort includes distribution of bilingual brochures, a series of coping skills workshops in Spanish, and cultural seminars directed at the Hispanic community.

Tucson Public Library publishes a "fotonovela"—"Leer es Poder!" (Reading Is Power). The "fotonovela," a story told with photographs and word balloons, is a favored popular reading format among Hispanics worldwide. For further information about these programs, contact:

> Queens Borough Public Library, 8911 Merrick Blvd, Jamaica, NY 11432
> Tucson Public Library, P.O. Box 27470, Tucson, AZ 85726-7470

Another tried and true technique to reach nonusers is through their group affiliations. Knowledge of various community groups is necessary, as is the ability to present material that is of high interest to the group. *The image of a friendly, nonthreatening community library will be essential in any appeal to nonusers.*

With the ever-increasing older population, libraries need to evaluate services offered to senior citizens. Historically, little effort has been directed at this group. Imaginative, creative programs, such as those offered to children, can also be developed for the elderly.

VIDEOCASSETTES AND TAPES

No consensus exists about offering videocassettes as a library service. With the proliferation of home videocassette recorders, this service certainly has the ability to attract new users. The chief drawbacks are the potential for competition with local videocassette stores and the initial expense of purchasing videocassettes for the library's collection. In reality, actual cost per circulation is lower than for most books. Certainly a regional circuit would decrease costs and increase variety. If your library is interested in providing videos, be wary of purchasing only educational or classical topics. On the other hand, David L. Leamon reports that "our non-entertainment videos move at practically the same pace as our entertainment videos."[5]

Tape cassettes, particularly children's tapes, are well-used. Children's tapes are quite inexpensive in relation to cost per circulation. However, problems with damage and keeping the accompanying program booklet and tape together will create headaches. Some libraries deal only with children's tapes and do not get involved with adult music tapes, language tapes, or audio books. Major jobbers, such as Baker & Taylor and Bowker, now carry a variety of video and audio cassettes. Selection policies will be determined by space, budget, interlibrary loan accessibility, and changing needs.

BOOK SELECTION AND WEEDING

Much has been written about book selection. However, every librarian will probably have a slightly different philosophy because so many factors influence selection. The debate over selection by demand versus traditional book selection criteria should concern all public librarians. Because my library receives donations of 1,000 books a month and because of rigid space constraints, *adult fiction* selection of donated material as well as weeding is often based only on the copyright date (1980 or later) and appeal of the physical book. Of course the collection does include recognized classics.

Most community librarians have time constraints and/or a very limited budget when they are selecting and purchasing books. Traditional selections through library review journals may be an overwhelming task in the very small library. Realistically, the innumerable bibliographies published by various organizations can serve as the basis for 90 percent of the library's collection. Use of these bibliographies ensures that the selection is the best available material in the field as reviewed by persons with appropriate expertise. Each community also has needs for material that only the librarian with knowledge of that community's needs can select, although *Public Library Catalog* will often review the very title that you need. Bestsellers, which appear on the *New York Times* bestseller list, can be purchased quickly through local bookstores or by telephone using toll-free numbers. By reading book reviews that appear in *Time* or *Newsweek*, the librarian will be aware of current books in which the community is interested.

> We believe in the power of a book to shape the life of an individual. It's natural, therefore, to expect that libraries will offer only edifying material, especially the classics. The reality, as we all know, is that

most folks pass us by. "A classic," Twain tartly observed, "is a book which people praise and don't read." We may offer nutritious fare—high carbohydrate, high fiber nonfiction and low fat, low sodium novels—but most of the public goes for junk food.[6]

Weeding the collection with a heavy hand will benefit the clientele, the staff, the library's image, and even the bookshelves. Many community libraries could dispose of much of their collection without getting rid of material that is actually used. Study after study shows that weeding actually increases book circulation.

Borrowers in large public libraries select approximately 50 percent of their material by browsing. The percentage increases as the collection decreases in size. Perhaps as much as 90 percent of selection is made by the browsing method in community libraries. A selective collection allows the user to find desirable and timely material more readily. The books are far more appealing. The staff does not spend needless time shifting unused books, nor is the catalog full of cards that have no purpose. *Learn to be very, very selective.*

REFERENCE SERVICE

Reference is probably the most difficult quality service to provide from a small public library. It requires a broader, more extensive collection than can usually be afforded, and it requires staff trained to know the contents of those reference books. However, in Maryland, a statewide reference study found that 82.5 percent of the questions could be answered from one of six sources:

> *World Almanac*
> *World Book Encyclopedia*
> *Information Please Almanac*
> *Stevenson's Home Book of Quotations*
> *Reader's Guide to Periodical Literature*
> Unabridged dictionary.[7]

Make sure that volunteers and the staff are familiar with the survey and the books above. Questions are often referred to the librarian that could be answered just as quickly and effectively by the staff. Many staff members have no confidence in their ability to answer even the simplest reference question. With experience, the staff will gain in confidence, and the librarian will gain a little time.

VERTICAL FILES

Vertical files can provide timely information at a nominal cost. Articles can be clipped selectively from magazines and newspapers. Material should either be placed on the appropriate shelf in pamphlet boxes or organized in a filing cabinet. Do not allow this service to grow out of control. Keep the mechanics very simple and weed with great vigor on a regular basis.

LITERACY PROGRAMS

Literacy programs fill a real need in many communities.

> For the nation as a whole nearly 13% of the population is illiterate or about one person in every eight. The English Language Proficiency Survey data showed that illiteracy is now a problem of the cities; whereas, previous studies had identified the problem as more serious in rural America. Among native English speaking adults in their twenties and thirties, illiteracy is ten times more prevalent than one would estimate using the tractional criterion of a sixth grade education."[8]

The library can provide an important community service by supplying both a meeting place for students and trained tutors and easy adult reading materials. In some states, federally funded literacy grants are available to qualifying libraries. *Libraries and Literacy*, by Debra Wilcox Johnson, covers the key points in developing a literacy program for the library.

BOOKMOBILES

Bookmobiles provide personal services and often have a small but very vocal group of supporters. Costs of the service can be high. "Like branches, bookmobiles too have a point of optimum service. Briefly it is that no stop should be continued if after a reasonable trial it fails to result in a rate of circulation of about a book a minute."[9] On the other hand, a bookmobile can be a highly visible promotional device for the entire library. The bookmobile can be a traveling billboard.

Give it a catchy name or slogan.

> *Follow the Reader*—North Central Saskatchewan Regional Library, Canada
> *The Rambling Rack*—Boliver County Library, MS
> *The Loan Ranger*—Santa Cruz, CA
> *Knowers Ark*—Freeport, NY.[10]

Promote the bookmobile with accurate and readable schedules. Do not try to have one schedule to cover all stops. Prominently display a sign

Have library, will travel

that states, "We will be back on _____ ." Gimmicks and a friendly image will be necessary to encourage nonusers to even step inside. Make unscheduled stops at parks, local events, and the lake.

Evaluation

Diversity in the library's collection and activities attracts new users and assures continued usage. However, some services will be heavily used and others will hardly be used at all. Traditionally, libraries have provided services, then looked for users. The order should obviously be reversed. Every service costs money and requires maintenance of effort, so learn to critique each activity carefully. Evaluation of fundraising activities and publicity releases has been covered in other chapters and therefore is not included here.

CHECKLIST FOR LIBRARY ACTIVITIES

On the checklist that appears as figure 3, evaluate activities *now offered* based on usage, on the staff time required, and on the special forms, extra handling, or unusual space allocations that are necessary. Just because a service requires ongoing publicity as well as considerable staff time does not mean that it should be eliminated. Well-attended storytimes provide an excellent example. On the other hand, a Wednesday afternoon storytime that regularly attracts less than five children might be rescheduled.

Complete the checklist of activities that the library currently offers (figure 3). You may be astonished at the length. Seriously consider eliminating those that are deadwood. Your time, your budget, and your library can only be divided so many ways.

CHECKLIST OF LIBRARY ACTIVITIES

Column A— Usage—Indicate H (High), M (Medium) or L (Low)
Column B— Use an X if special forms, high space allocation, or extra handling are required. (Circulation of a camera probably requires a special form. A record cannot be placed in the bookdrop.)
Column C— Staff Time—Place an X in this column if the item requires a high amount of staff time during processing, circulation, etc. (Films must be checked before they are recirculated.)
Column D— Star (*) the activities that you may want to eliminate.

	A	B	C	D

Special Collections

Adult fiction

Adult nonfiction

Art prints

Bestsellers

Caldecott winners

Camera

College catalogs

Easy readers

Fiction genre (mystery . . .)

Films

Filmstrips

Foreign languages

Genealogy

Juvenile fiction

Juvenile nonfiction

Large print books

Local history

(cont.)

Fig. 3.   Library checklist

Special Collections, cont.	A	B	C	D
Magazines				
Circulation	___	___	___	___
Research	___	___	___	___
Maps	___	___	___	___
Microfilm	___	___	___	___
Paperbacks	___	___	___	___
Phonograph records	___	___	___	___
Picture books	___	___	___	___
Reference	___	___	___	___
Tapes	___	___	___	___
Telephone books	___	___	___	___
Toys	___	___	___	___
Vertical files	___	___	___	___
Young adult	___	___	___	___

Programs

	A	B	C	D
Adult education classes	___	___	___	___
Book club	___	___	___	___
Book talks	___	___	___	___
Community events	___	___	___	___
Films	___	___	___	___
Junior Great Books	___	___	___	___
Library tours	___	___	___	___
Literacy programs	___	___	___	___
Puppet shows	___	___	___	___
Special displays (artist, woodcarver . . .)	___	___	___	___
Storytime	___	___	___	___
Summer reading program	___	___	___	___

Fig. 3. *(cont.)* Library checklist

	A	B	C	D
Services				
Bibliography booklets	____	____	____	____
Bookdrop	____	____	____	____
Bookmarks	____	____	____	____
Bookmobile	____	____	____	____
Card catalog	____	____	____	____
Community bulletin board	____	____	____	____
Community room	____	____	____	____
Copy machine	____	____	____	____
Coupon exchange	____	____	____	____
Delivery to shut-ins	____	____	____	____
Equipment loan				
Cassette player	____	____	____	____
Film projector/screen	____	____	____	____
Typewriter	____	____	____	____
Slide projector	____	____	____	____
VCR	____	____	____	____
Gift shop	____	____	____	____
Interlibrary loan	____	____	____	____
Newsletter	____	____	____	____
Paperback book exchange	____	____	____	____
Pattern exchange	____	____	____	____
Phone reference	____	____	____	____
Public restroom	____	____	____	____
Public telephone	____	____	____	____
Reader's advisory service	____	____	____	____
Reference	____	____	____	____
Reserves	____	____	____	____
Talks to outside groups	____	____	____	____
Tax forms	____	____	____	____
Used book sale	____	____	____	____

Fig. 3. *(cont.)* Library checklist

COMPARISON OF POTENTIAL ACTIVITIES

Before any decision is made to implement new activities, you need to be concerned about some very basic considerations. Utilize the chart shown in figure 4 to evaluate and compare various factors. The level of effort (low, moderate, high) should be used to rate the activity.

Criteria		*Level of Effort*		
Activity		#1	#2	#3
1. Staff hours needed to implement		____	____	____
2. Facilities needed to implement		____	____	____
3. Overall cost		____	____	____
4. Potential benefits for the library and the community		____	____	____
5. Objectives accomplished		____	____	____
6. Risk of failure		____	____	____
7. Other criteria		____	____	____

Fig. 4.   Comparison of potential activities

Conclusion

The relationship between the people of the community, the role of the library, and the services provided need to be evaluated carefully. These factors will be unique for each community. Having identified a need and provided a service, the library must now publicize the service's availability. Publicity and presentation of material are covered in Chapters 5 and 6.

Notes

1. Jim Fish, "Community Analysis," *Bay State Librarian*, 67 (June 1978): 17–19.
2. Douglas Zweizig, "Community Analysis," in *Local Public Library Administration*, 2nd ed., ed. by Ellen Altman (Chicago: American Library Association, 1980), 42.

3. Susan E. Brandehoff, "The 'ideal' public library—videocassettes a top priority," *American Libraries*, 17 (December 1986): 859.

4. Marian S. Edsall, *Library Promotion Handbook* (Phoenix: Oryx, 1980), 123.

5. David L. Leamon, "No Fees for Services," *Library Administrator's Digest*, 12 (June 1987): 46.

6. Bob Gaines, "Collection Management Notes," *Central Texas Library System Newsletter* (March 1987): 1–3.

7. Nancy Bolt and Corrine Johnson, *Options for Small Public Libraries in Massachusetts* (Chicago: American Library Association, 1985), 40.

8. Susan Hildebrand, "Texas at Bottom in Literacy," *Library Developments*, 8 (August 1986): 4.

9. Joseph L. Wheeler and Herbert Goldhor, *Practical Administration of Public Libraries* (New York: Harper and Row, 1962), 426.

10. Edsall, 149.

Recommended Reading

Baeckler, Virginia, and Linda Larson. *GO, PEP, and POP!* New York: The Unabashed Librarian, 1976.

Edsall, Marian S. *Library Promotion Handbook*. Phoenix: Oryx, 1980.

Johnson, Debra Wilcox. *Libraries and Literacy*. Chicago: American Library Association, 1987.

Liebold, Louise Condak. *Fireworks, Brass Bands and Elephants*. Phoenix: Oryx, 1986.

Zweizig, Douglas. "Community Analysis." In *Local Public Library Administration*, edited by Ellen Altman. 2nd ed. Chicago: American Library Association, 1980.

Chapter 3

PANNING FOR GOLD

Funding problems plague most community libraries. Small libraries operate on a bizarre conglomeration of governmental funds, individual donations, monies obtained through fundraising activities, and grants.

> The average donation from individuals and groups (in 1981) was $475. Of this amount, churches brought in the most, $313, education $45, hospitals $37 and other health concerns $64. Since libraries are grouped with education, it is obvious that they have not made the mark. Recognizing that a tremendous amount of money is donated annually in the United States, libraries of all sizes and types should begin investigating ways of acquiring their fair share.[1]

As if the poor showing of libraries is not enough cause for concern, estimates are that "more than $33 billion in government funding, according to the Urban Institute, will be lost to the nonprofit sector throughout the mid-1980s."[2]

Overview of Fundraising

The term fundraising is used throughout this book to refer to funding of any kind for the library. While funding refers primarily to cash, it can also include donations of equipment, services, bonds, bequests, property, and even livestock. A West Texas library recently received a donation of the prize bull from the local fair. A live animal is not a typical gift, but the bull was worth $900. As a rule of thumb, it is far easier to acquire donated equipment or services than cash.

PERSONAL CONTACTS

All fundraising has certain characteristics in common. Personal contacts are a must—*ask and ask and ask some more*. Requesting money from people and businesses can be a very positive form of public relations. People are more aware of the library's existence and needs if they have been personally contacted. Involve everyone. Whether a person makes a cake for the cake walk, sits in a dunking booth, or helps make posters is immaterial. A person who is involved on any level is far more likely to become a supporter than one who has never had any dealings with the library.

Two key elements are to find the right person to do the asking and to find the right person to ask. *It is important to ask the right person for the right amount the first time around.* This cannot be done unless careful planning has gone into the campaign. "Funds are not in fact raised. They are solicited, requested, demanded, cajoled, enticed, and inveigled."[3] Once people have donated money, no matter whether it is $1, $100 or $1000, they will feel that they have done their fair share. This librarian still shudders to think of the flyer distributed by the Westbank Community Library during its early stages that stated that "for just $1 per person we could have a local library."

RECOGNITION

Promptly recognize the person or organization donating money. At a minimum, write appropriate letters of appreciation. Avoid form letters. A compromise to an impersonal letter could include a quick handwritten note at the bottom. Try to publicize large donations through photographs or newspaper articles. Many donors hope to be publicly recognized for their gifts. Awareness of one donation may well trigger another.

The image that the library projects will be critical to successful fundraising. A dynamic, involved library stands a better chance of receiving funds, since donors are far more likely to give money to a successful operation. Government entities will also be more likely to support an organization that they think the people want.

Fundraising, whether through events, direct appeal, or large donor solicitation, requires energy and time commitments from the librarian, the board, and the volunteers. Be very wary of events that are not profitable.

The Library Board

Securing funds for the library is the board's primary function. The innocuous term *fundraising* describes an endless list of activities covering events, grant applications, and donations of services, furnishings, cash, and investments. To provide appropriate funds, *the library board continually lobbies for money.* Effective and timely presentations to governmental entities ensure better funding.

Often overlooked and sadly underrated, the nominating committee provides the key to board personnel and future growth. Board members should be selected based on their ties to the social, cultural, religious, professional, ethnic, and business circles in the community. Besides being strong, caring personalities, members also need to be *tactful* and discreet. Future board members, before accepting the nomination, need to have a clear idea of the number of hours and meetings per month that will be required and should be provided with a written job description.

Securing funds is the board's most important responsibility

No matter how the library is funded, the current level of fiscal responsibility, as well as long-term plans, will directly correlate with the involvement and concern of the board. The sources of money will vary greatly depending on historical precedent and geographical location. A large percentage of community libraries, however, will receive money from a variety of sources. Even though the community library is funded by a government entity or through an endowment fund, this should not prevent the board from seeking other funds. Very few libraries provide maximum service to their community in adequately staffed buildings. Furthermore, many communities have been or will be affected by federal, state, and local cuts in government payrolls.

The librarian may create awareness of specific needs, but the enthusiasm and commitment for any successful increase in funds lies with the board. Many nonprofit organizations consider the most important trait of a board member to be his or her ability and willingness to raise money. If fundraising is a subject of dread to the board, some basic concepts of board responsibilities need to be addressed. In larger communities, seminars are available that deal with board development. If courses arc not available in your community, the board might consider hiring a consultant to teach them fundraising techniques. With few exceptions, board members intend to provide the community with a valuable service. Some boards, however, get bogged down in minor issues and are either unaware of or unwilling to face the critical problem of fundraising, which is the key to a library's survival.

A recent report describes the criteria of the board of trustees for a successful small public library as one that

> Participates in the determination of the purpose and direction of the library;
>
> Hires the best librarian it can afford for library director rather than the cheapest person it can get;
>
> Advocates full funding of public library services;
>
> Takes advantage of opportunities to learn about libraries and issues relating to libraries;
>
> Seeks funds, in cooperation with the library director and community groups, creatively and on an ongoing basis.[4]

Notice that three out of five of the above elements deal with funding concerns. Many successful boards require that members approach a minimum number of people each month to solicit support. Some boards even require identification of the person(s) contacted at monthly board meetings. Over an extended period, this method of one-on-one fundraising produces astonishing results.

The entire issue of board accountability, whether dealing with fundraising, attendance, or insurance problems, is a sticky one. Accountability can assist the members to become a more effective board. Depending on the diplomacy of the president, accountability can either create feelings of ill will or it can be viewed as positive reinforcement for a difficult assignment. After all, even the least effective board member gives his or her time and energy. Most board members genuinely aspire to being a positive force in the organization.

Community Organizations

A basic understanding of the community's structure is necessary in order to make intelligent monetary decisions affecting the library. A community is both a political system and a social system with shared mutual interests. The library is one of hundreds of organizations in a typical community. How effectively the library interacts with other organizations and its leaders will directly affect funding decisions. "Before the public library can implement a plan that affects the community, it must have the support sanction of those organization leaders who control large amounts of resources and who make up what is called the power structure of the community."[5]

SECTORS OF THE COMMUNITY

Organizational Structure

Edward Howard divides organizations into four groups: government, independent, private, and voluntary.[6] Governmental entities include local, regional, state, and federal organizations. Independent groups are nonprofit, tax-exempt service organizations. The business community, predicated on profit, forms the private sector. *An often overlooked fact is that the private sector is the primary support for the other three sectors.* The voluntary group is composed of people who share a common interest or purpose. Most libraries will fall into either the governmental or the independent sectors. Typical organizations are listed in the following chart.

Voluntary Sector

Genealogical Society	Rotary Club
Community Theater	Humane Society
League of Women Voters	Toastmasters Club
Medical Society Auxiliary	Churches
Democratic Women's Club	PTA
Bar Association	Reading Club

Government Sector

Social Security Administration	Postal Service
Internal Revenue Service	Congressional Offices
License Bureau	Co-op Extension Service
Highway Department	Police
Junior college	Zoning board
Fire Department	Orphan's home
Civil Defense	Mayor
Public schools	Tax Assessor

Independent Sector

Hospital	Senior citizens centers
YMCA	Salvation Army
Girl Scouts	Chamber of Commerce
Day care centers	American Red Cross

Private Sector

Retail and service trades	Medical services
Transportation	Construction

Finance   Utilities
Agribusiness   Communication

INTERDEPENDENCE

All community organizations compete with one another and are also
interdependent.

> The public library in a very real sense is in competition with every
> other organization in the community, particularly those in its own
> sector. It follows, then, that the library administration is engaged in a
> competitive match with the chief executives of other organizations.
> And like others of the games people play, this competition can be
> light-hearted and friendly or serious and destructive.[7]

Because the library needs allies to support its own ends, it cooperates
with other organizations that also need allies. This cooperation is basic to
organizational survival. Organizations can either approve or disapprove
of the library programs and budget. A clear need exists for developing
relationships with leaders of various groups.

POWER STRUCTURE

Every community has a power structure. Identification of the key players
is a must, since these extremely powerful leaders make decisions in
three or even four different organizations. The most powerful players are
not necessarily officers in an organization nor do their names appear in
the paper. They are often wealthy, and they are usually longtime residents of the community. The positive support of these key players will
almost guarantee success. Conversely, their opposition will often ensure
defeat.

> Influencing the outcome of community decision-making is a highly
> complex process involving communication, exchange, bargaining,
> compromise, conflicts and trade-offs. Large numbers proclaim they
> are interested in community affairs, but few turn out for the practice
> sessions, either as participants or as spectators. Fewer still are those
> who actually play. Most researchers fix the number at less than one
> percent in the average community. The apathy of members of an
> organization permits the organization leader to make decisions of
> considerable import.[8]

To identify the interorganizational leaders, first compile a list of all
organizations, then identify all persons who have decision-making posi-

tions. The names that appear on several lists will be *key players*. The next task is to analyze how well you or a board member knows each person and to develop a strategy for strengthening these ties.

The importance of the library within the community structure has been sadly undervalued by librarians and library boards for many years. A ridiculous situation exists where the public perceives the library as an important element of the community, but the librarian and the board do not. Participation by the librarian and the board in the community's power structure is a feasible and effective way to ensure adequate funding.

Fundraising

Fundraising should be well-planned, since poorly planned fundraising will almost assuredly fail. The infamous who, what, where, when, why, and how need to be dealt with and resolved before any actual fundraising occurs.

COMMON DENOMINATORS

Who?

Who is responsible for coordinating and implementing the campaign— the board, the Friends, the staff, the cleaning crew? Establish very clear lines of authority, such as who makes the day-to-day decision, who authorizes any expenditures, who keeps what records, and who reports to whom. The clearer the lines of accountability, the more productive people will be. The leader of the fundraising effort will be critical to its success. *The right person needs to be a community leader who understands the community organization, who is enthusiastic, who is a decision maker, and who is willing to make a financial commitment.*

What?

What amount of money do you need to raise? On what will the money be spent? Define your goals. Is this a one-time campaign for a specific item, or will it need to be ongoing for recurring expenses?

Where?

Where can you get the money? Evaluate the type of fundraising which will most effectively meet your needs. Grants, special events (fairs, dinners, book sales), direct appeal, corporate giving, and government sources are the five basic choices. Each has definite advantages and limitations. The larger the donation, the more clearly the goals need to be stated. People will not give large gifts to a poorly planned fundraising campaign.

When?

When should you begin fundraising? Start planning your campaign as soon as you identify the need. No action means no money. Once you initiate a plan, set well defined deadlines. Enthusiasm wanes as fund-raising drags on.

Why?

Why does the library need money? A clear case must be presented. Prepare carefully documented explanations for areas of probable opposi-tion *before* the opposition is organized. Every benefit needs to be listed and reinforced with statistics, whether it is applied to a new building or increased operating funds. The larger the fundraising goal, the more elaborate the case statement needs to be. A case statement for a capital campaign should include a title page, a summary, a budget, and support statements.

Why do donors give money? Potential donors usually give money to benefit themselves in some way. Tax benefits, public recognition, an investment in the future, an opportunity for a permanent memorial, and provision of a cultural resource for the community are the most common reasons for giving. A clear understanding by board members of potential benefits is essential. Never assume that a donor is already aware of these benefits.

How?

How can you be assured of success? If your only criterion is reaching a dollar goal, you cannot be guaranteed of success. If, however, the library creates a well-planned effort which is enthusiastically supported by your whole organization, you are guaranteed of increased community aware-ness and support for the library. You may have to sponsor another event to reach your goal, but you have already laid a great deal of groundwork and will benefit from this in the future.

FUNDRAISING INCOME

Fundraising exhausts volunteers, board members, and librarians at an alarming rate. Before any commitment is made to a potential fundraising activity, be very sure it is worth the energy and time that it will assuredly consume. See the sample estimates in figure 5.

SAMPLE—BOOK SALE

Workers needed
> To organize event—sort, price, move—10
> To work that day—4 people in 2 hour shifts = 8
>> Total = 18 people

Rough estimate of expenses
> Dollars that have to be guaranteed to caterer, etc.—$50 for tent; $25 for flyers & posters
>> Total = $75

Maximum number of attendees
> Does this appeal to appropriate audience?—yes
> How will they be reached?—articles, flyers
> Worst scenario (minimum number of attendees)—unknown

The bottom line—Expectations of net proceeds—$400

SAMPLE—BARBECUE DINNER

Workers needed
> To organize event—3
> To work that day—2 per 2-hour shift for tickets; 4 for cleanup = 8
>> Total = 11 people

Rough estimate of expenses
> Dollars that have to be guaranteed to caterer, etc.—500 meals at $3.50 each—$1,750; flyers—$25
>> Total = $1,775

Maximum number of attendees
> Does this appeal to appropriate audience?—Yes, during rodeo
> How will they be reached?—articles, flyers, people attending rodeo
> Worst scenario (minimum number of attendees)—500 people

The bottom line—Expectations of net proceeds
> Dinner sales 700 at $6 apiece = $4200 less expenses: $2425
>   500 at $6 apiece = $3000 less expenses: $1225

Fig. 5. Sample estimates of fundraising profits; book sale and barbeque

Estimate of Fundraising Profits

The following breakdown allows a quick and easy method of analyzing income from any potential fundraising activity:

Workers needed
> To organize event
> To work that day
>> Total =

Rough estimate of expenses
    Dollars that have to be guaranteed to caterer, etc.
        Total =

Maximum number of attendees
    Does this appeal to appropriate audience?
    How will they be reached?
    Worst scenario (minimum number of attendees)

The bottom line—Expectations of net proceeds

Fundraiser coordinator

TYPES OF FUNDRAISERS

Each funding agency or fundraising event has advantages and disadvantages. Special events, direct appeals, major campaigns, grants, corporate giving, and governmental sources are all considered fundraisers.

Special Events

Pros: Opportunity for lots of publicity
        Direct involvement of large numbers of people
        Attraction of nonusers and people from outside the community
            who would not otherwise participate
        Promotion of community spirit

Cons: Substantial number of workers needed
        Months of planning and execution needed
        High expense to income ratio
        Potential area of volunteer "burnout"

Special events provide a time-honored way for libraries to raise money. In small communities, these events rarely raise more than $5,000 and quite often raise only $500. While events almost always draw attention to the library and create community goodwill, they can also be very time-consuming, requiring substantial amounts of volunteer time. Be very careful that the monetary gain or the gain in visibility justifies the energy that is expended.

    Libraries have probably been holding book sales since the first library opened. Some different approaches for book sales might be to sell books by the pound, to sell books by the inch, or to sell bags of books for a dollar. Have a high school government class that needs service hours deliver the books to the sale location and return them to the storage area after the sale. Give excess books to the county jail. Give away excess books as a "freebie." Have an ongoing book sale in an unused part of the library. The more organized the book collection, the more popular the sale. Throw away 90 percent of the unused magazines and 100 percent of the condensed books. Do not keep items that will not sell. Borrow a tent from the local undertaker in which to hold the book sale. You will have shade, and he will get free advertising.

Many community libraries participate in an annual carnival or fair. Here are some tips to increase your chances of success:

> *Keep your expenses down!* Draw up a budget of anticipated costs and try to come in under budget. Compare prices and ask for donations. The difference of a few pennies in the cost of carnival prizes multiplied by hundreds will make a big difference in your profit.
>
> *Use your community resources.* Local celebrities will often participate if they are asked. Area businesses and organizations will give help and advice. They will often loan needed equipment. Let your needs be known before you purchase anything. Every dollar saved is one less you need to raise.
>
> *Keep careful records.* Evaluate the effectiveness of your campaign and examine problems by keeping detailed notes. These records can be invaluable when repeating a similar event.
>
> *Be creative.* Give a new twist to an old idea. Your community will be more likely to respond to a fresh approach. Even if you repeat last year's event, give it a new theme and a catchy title.
>
> *Don't be afraid to use humor.* You want *your* appeal to stand out from all the rest. People like to smile.

Art shows, home tours, barbecue dinners, pancake breakfasts, raffles, bingo, 5K runs, street dances, raft races, book talks, riverboat rides, rodeos, and concerts are only a few of the ways libraries raise money through special events. The list is apparently endless.

Direct Appeal

Pros: Effectiveness of personal contact
Low expenses if volunteers are used
Quick results

Cons: High number of workers needed
Reluctance of people to directly approach others to ask for money

Catch people's attention

Direct appeal fundraising can be done by mail, by telephone, or by personal contact in door-to-door solicitation. It can be an effective and positive fundraising method. Except in the case of direct mail, costs are nominal. Even if a person who receives a direct appeal does not make a contribution, she or he is made aware that a community library exists and that the library has funding concerns.

The Westbank Community Library ran a series of highly successful phone banks as part of a building campaign. Because the phone bank was so successful, the script and follow-up have been adapted for use by any library. Callers worked with a very short script, which asked a series of questions.

> Hi, I'm _____ , one of your neighbors calling to ask for your support for the _____ Community Library. Are you familiar with the library?

> The library was created and funded by your friends and neighbors. _____ (city, county, etc.) gives the library $ _____ each year, but all other money must be raised through donations. All contributions are tax deductible.

> It costs $ _____ to operate the library for one year. We have a number of categories of giving. Would you like to give $ _____ to operate the library for one week? (Wait for answer.) Or $ _____ for one day? (Wait for answer.) Or $ _____ for one hour? (Wait for answer.)

It was far more effective not to read the script but to talk naturally. People were more receptive if they answered questions throughout the conversation. Individuals who had never been in the library were willing to give money! Even if the person did not make a donation, enormous public awareness was created. Besides raising over $90,000, the library attracted seven new volunteers, generated innumerable book donations, and added at least twenty-five new borrowers.

The follow-up communication entailed much more work than anticipated. Letters were sent to those who indicated they might make a contribution. A significant number of persons who had not made a positive commitment over the phone did send money. The letters should be sent promptly; they will probably qualify for bulk mailing rates. Each person was sent an information sheet about the library as well as the letter shown in figure 6 on the library's letterhead.

Major Campaign

Pros: Raises a large sum of money in a limited time.
        Focuses attention on the permanency of the library as a community resource.

Cons: Requires experienced leadership for the campaign or the campaign must absorb cost of a professional fundraiser.
        Momentum is lost if not completed in a timely manner.

When a library needs to raise funds to build a new library, remodel an older building, establish an endowment fund, or purchase new furnish-

YES! I want our community library to stay open. Enclosed is my check for:

$52,000 for 1 year*

$1,000 for 1 week   Name _____

$200 for 1 day   Address _____

$100 for ½ day   _____

$25 for 1 hour   Phone _____

Other

*See us for convenient installment plan!

Community energy and enthusiasm created a library for our area. Your tax deductible gift assures that our dream will become a reality. Together, we will build a library of which we can all be proud.

Make check payable to: Westbank Community Library
                         2224 Walsh Tarlton
                         Austin, Texas 78746

Fig. 6. Follow-up letter for donation

ings, a major campaign is usually necessary. The key elements—who, what, where, why, how—must be carefully planned and developed for a major fundraising campaign. Be aware of potential problems and objections. Prepare explanations before the campaign begins and before the opposition is organized. After the case statement is prepared and the campaign chairperson is selected, potential donors must be identified, and the size of the gift that they are able to make must be estimated. *Even if you hire a professional fundraiser, this is the first task that will be assigned to the board.*

Literature on major fundraising stresses again and again that the way money is raised is based on the structure of a pyramid. Ninety percent of the donations will be received from 10 percent of the donors. If the goal is $100,000, the gifts received might look like this:

> one gift of $25,000
> two gifts of $10,000 each
> five gifts of $5,000 each
> ten gifts of $1,000 each
> twenty gifts of $500 each
> many small gifts totaling $10,000.

For any major fundraising campaign, such as raising money to build a new wing for the library, individual board members *must* support the effort financially. Professional fundraisers expect that 30 percent of the total goal will be contributed by board members. This information will come as a shock to many boards. Very possibly it is a goal that will not be feasible to meet. On the other hand, the campaign will definitely be affected by the board's inability or unwillingness to make a financial commitment. If a major campaign looms in your future, consider adding wealthy potential donors to your board. Remember that membership on the library board, no matter what the size of the community, should be an honor as well as a public recognition of one's commitment to the library.

Large gifts of money can be effectively solicited only by persons who have already made large donations. A positive approach to potential donors might be to say, "I gave $5,000 to the library fund, and I hope that you will do the same." People who are in a position to donate large amounts of money already know that this strategy is often used and will probably be willing to ask their friends for a similar donation.

If you ask a donor for $100 instead of $10,000, you will rarely be able to go back and correct your mistake. *A person who gives money feels that he or she has done his or her fair share after one contribution.*

Fundraisers need to be given a time frame in which to ask for donations, since they tend to procrastinate. They need to be able to state how a potential donor can help in very clear terms. Donors have to be asked on an individual basis. Stress that gifts of land, stock, bonds, and property are desirable and acceptable. Bequests that are part of an estate or trust can provide tax benefits and are a practical alternative to an immediate gift. Attorneys and insurance agents are in an ideal position to promote the community library as the recipient of bequests.

If widespread community involvement in building or expanding the library is desirable, consider establishing a building fund committee. *Members should be selected because they are influential and have the time, money, and energy to give to the library.* As people are asked to join the committee, they should be very aware this is a *fundraising* committee, not a titular or advisory position. Goals and a time frame should be established before the group is formed. At the first meeting, assignments for contacts should be made. People do not want to discuss and dissect fundraising goals. *Do not waste their time.* They want an appropriate assigned task that can be accomplished in a reasonable period of time. Then they want to forget about fundraising for the library.

Another alternative is to host a series of breakfasts, luncheons, or dinners for selected guests. The speaker must present a very clear message—*the library is important to his or her personal life.* Many well-known authors and politicians can be quite eloquent on the importance of a library in their life today or when they were children. The guests need to be told specifically how they can help. Present various options. Try to match a person's interests with the library needs. Money given in memory of a loved one has provided funds for numerous libraries. Many people are fascinated by new technology and might be interested in providing funds for computer equipment. Someone interested in communications might fund a "community center" that would enable you to display notices, store forms, and provide a community bulletin board. A children's room could be named after a donor's grandchild. Libraries have many different needs which can be presented so that they appeal to a wide variety of people.

Grants

Pros: Single source for a relatively large donation
        Preparation of the application requires only one or two people

Cons: Expertise required for grant writing
        Time-consuming documentation
        Long response time
        Chances of receiving any but local grants slim

Many people will suggest that you apply for grants. However, after submitting over 200 grant proposals in three years, this librarian thinks that grants as a source of *major* funds are sadly overrated. Small grants in the $500–$3000 range are more readily available.

Your best chance for obtaining a grant will be from a *local* foundation. Awareness of the various possibilities in your immediate vicinity is a must. Foundation directories can be helpful, but they often do not include small, local foundations. Many large businesses have foundations which make money available in geographic areas where they have a franchise or chain store. Utility companies often support foundations. With any luck, there may be an enormous endowment fund set up just to benefit your community.

After investigating local resources, check on regional and statewide foundations. As a last resort, try national foundations. Foundation directories will be helpful in all of these areas. Foundations receive zillions of requests for money. In order to be considered by one of the larger endowment funds, those libraries requesting funding need to be very unusual or to involve a foundation board member personally. Those involved in fundraising for the library need to search their memories for potential foundation board members.

After identifying likely prospects, write and ask for guidelines with a *brief* letter on the library letterhead. Include a short statement of your funding needs. (See figure 7.) A fair number of likely prospects may reject your application at this point. You can reduce the chances of this by carefully following any suggested format, putting the information in the order requested, paying attention to the number of copies required, and meeting any deadlines. While it is not necessary to hire a professional grant writer to prepare proposals, the applications should still look neat and be presented competently. Once again, it is the image of the library that is being evaluated.

If you make many grant applications, you will be grateful for a copy machine. *Keep a copy of the proposal for your files.* Not only will you have a copy in case of follow-up questions, but you may find the information useful to keep for future reference.

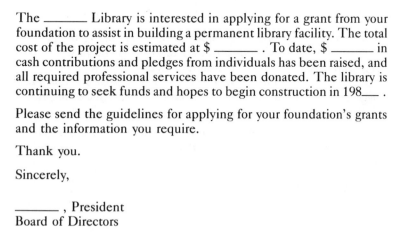

Gentlemen:

The _____ Library is interested in applying for a grant from your foundation to assist in building a permanent library facility. The total cost of the project is estimated at $ _____ . To date, $ _____ in cash contributions and pledges from individuals has been raised, and all required professional services have been donated. The library is continuing to seek funds and hopes to begin construction in 198___ .

Please send the guidelines for applying for your foundation's grants and the information you require.

Thank you.

Sincerely,

_____ , President
Board of Directors

Fig. 7.   Letter of interest to a foundation

Corporate Giving

Pros: Needs few workers
        Opportunity to meet key business people in the community
        A good way to solicit in-kind donations or donations of interest to
            a specific business

Cons: Gifts usually limited to a specific service or piece of equipment

Corporate giving has only recently been recognized as a viable source of
funds for nonprofit organizations. Corporate giving generally refers to
gifts of services, equipment, or money from a business operating in the
area served by the library. The business is usually one of the more
successful ones in the area and, in fact, is often a branch of a large
corporation. Many of these businesses now allocate a specific amount of
money to benefit their local community each year. They do this both to
increase their corporate visibility and to provide a means of community
outreach. The businesses may be very concerned about how their gifts
are administered and will need to be reassured that the library practices
sound fiscal management. The request often needs to pinpoint a specific
need, and as such, the gift will be restricted to that designated item or
service. Actual examples are donation of a card catalog by a grocery store,
accounting services by a CPA firm, and a cash donation to underwrite the
cost of buying best-sellers by a dental office. The money may be auto-

Ladies and Gentlemen:

The _____ Library has been an integral part of our community for
the past _____ years. Our library is visited by _____ people and
circulates _____ books each year. *(Might include 1 or 2 more sentences
that reinforce the importance of the library to the community.)*

The library receives _____ percent of its operating budget from
_____ (city/county), but all other funds must be raised through
donations. At this time, the library needs help in purchasing a
_____ for the children's area. *(Possibly enclose a picture from a catalog.)* The entire cost for the item is $ _____ , including freight
charges.

Is there any possibility that your business could help us purchase this
item? We can certainly assure you that we would make your generos-
ity known in the community.

Sincerely,

President
_____ Library Board

Fig. 8.   Letter for corporate giving

matically allocated each year if the need is for a recurring service. Usually, however, the request must be made annually in writing.

Corporate gifts are often made to create goodwill within the community. Therefore it is extremely important to recognize these donations with news coverage, letters of appreciation, and verbal acknowledgment. *If the donation is received year after year, then the acknowledgments must also be made year after year.*

Corporate gifts can be solicited through letters or personal contact (see figure 8). The executive officer of one business contacting the officer of another business is certainly the most effective approach. A board member who is well-known and respected in the community makes a very powerful advocate. In any case, the person making the request should be well-informed about the library's history and needs. While solicitations can be made by letter, this will not be as effective as direct contact.

One library found that requests made in the fall brought double benefits. Some businesses still had unspent funds from the current year and were also willing to budget a library donation for the following year.

Government Funding

Pros: Provides ongoing, stable source of operating funds
        Potential opportunity to influence the final decision

Cons: Problems inherent in funding from a bureaucracy
        Must compete with all other publicly funded programs

Cities, townships, school districts, counties, states, and the federal government support community libraries. The degree and level of funding vary wildly. Many libraries are supported by a combination of funds from several different entities. A nationwide survey of rural libraries in towns serving no more than 25,000 people showed that 80 percent of all funds came from local municipalities, townships, and counties. State and federal funds accounted for just under 12 percent. A surprising number of libraries receive little or no financial support at the local level.[9] *The following paragraphs should encourage you, no matter what the past history, to actively pursue government funding.*

An attitude of resignation seems disturbingly widespread. Many libraries never attempt to obtain or increase local funds. The assumptions that no funds are available, that the elected officials would not even consider a request, and that voters would disapprove are commonly heard but are rarely supported by hard evidence.

> In a survey of people in East Central Illinois who are untaxed for public library service, 51% said they would vote "yes" for a library property tax referendum. The study related certain demographic characteristics to a probable "yes" vote for library service taxes. Nonproperty owners, small property owners, young married couples without children, couples with school-aged children, younger adults, and men were more likely to vote yes.[10]

The same energy that is expended on fundraising events, if directed towards securing government funding, might provide a far more satisfactory long-term solution. Understanding the community's power structure and making it work for you can prevent the annual budget crisis. One of the key recommendations from *Options for Small Public Libraries in Massachusetts* is that local library funds should equal at least 2 percent of the town's operating budget.[11]

COMMUNICATION   To assume that funding for a library will be a primary concern for government officials is naive. Many worthwhile causes hope to receive or increase their governmental funding. A continual public relations campaign is necessary to reinforce what each official already believes as well as to educate new officials about library needs. *Never assume that someone else is taking care of this.* Strong supporters of the library can and should be sent letters of appreciation well in advance of election campaigns. Elected representatives should personally know the librarian and the board president. Politics involves influence and the influential. Success in obtaining government funding will be determined by the relationship between the library administration and the local power structure. Identify the key figures in community decisions, get to know them personally, establish lines of communication, and let them know about library concerns. Work to assure their cooperation and support. This is an ongoing project that the entire board and the library staff should try to achieve. To repeat: *you* need to know and be recognized by all community leaders. When the library has a concern about funding or future growth, communication is the only way to resolve issues.

HEARINGS   Many libraries are represented at government hearings only once a year—during the annual budget review. Needless to say, this may give the government officials a narrow view of the library as a "taker." To avoid this, appear regularly. Know the officials by name. Present short, interesting facts about the community library. Give the officials copies of the more interesting handouts. Tell them about the high usage of the library during the summer or the success of a recent program. Quote pleased borrowers. Keep awareness of library activities high throughout the year.

Be in a position through your community contacts to prevent budget cuts. Encourage other community organizations to support library funding. Document increased needs in a professional manner. If necessary, prepare a packet for a budget proposal. Present it to individual officials before the actual hearing and go over any troublesome issues in a private meeting. An elected official often makes a public statement that he or she feels obligated to stand behind. Plan the best approach well in advance of budget hearings and then take time to implement the strategy. In the long run, government funding is by far the most desirable means of support.

SCHOOL DISTRICTS   Many state laws allow school districts to provide funding for public libraries. The correlation and relationship between the educational system and the community library are obvious. A library that works closely with teachers, the school administration, and the students will stand a far greater chance of obtaining funds. Remember that school districts often have surplus land, furniture, and sometimes even buildings that could be used by the community library.

FEDERAL FUNDING   Since the 1950s, the federal government has provided funds through the Library Services and Construction Act (LSCA). The LSCA funds have been used primarily for continuing programs and special projects. Continuing programs encompass support for regional systems, interlibrary loan networks, and direct aid. Special project funding, often in the form of matching grants, has been used for library construction, cooperation between different types of libraries, and services to the disadvantaged. Information about the grants is available from your state library.

EVALUATION

You may expend an enormous amount of energy, put in an exhausting day, and be left with a feeling of indebtedness to every one of your acquaintances, yet *the* fundraising event has raised only a nominal sum of money. Evaluating potential net income should be the most important aspect of preliminary planning. Evaluating the outcome of the event is equally important. Were estimates of profits, expenses, and personnel accurate? What could have been done to improve profit? Did the fundraiser reach its goal? Remember to evaluate increased awareness of the library that has resulted from advance publicity, the involvement of various individuals, and the actual event.

Conclusion

Funding is an extremely serious and apparently endless concern for all community libraries. Funding should be the top priority of every board member. Librarians and board members need to reevaluate their current approach to money problems. Participation in the local power structure can ensure permanent solutions to current funding needs and allow input into community decisions.

Notes

1. Pamela G. Bonnell, *Fund Raising for the Small Library* (Chicago: American Library Association, 1983), 1.
2. Fred Setterberg and Kary Schulman, *Beyond Profit: The Complete Guide to Managing the Nonprofit Organization* (New York: Harper and Row, 1985), 171.
3. Setterberg, 106.
4. Nancy Bolt and Corrine Johnson, *Options for Small Public Libraries in Massachusetts* (Chicago: Public Library Association, 1985), 55.
5. Edward N. Howard, *Local Power and the Community Library* (Chicago: American Library Association, 1978), 2.
6. Ibid., 12–15.
7. Ibid., 18.
8. Ibid., 25–26.
9. John W. Head, "The National Rural Library Reference Survey," *RQ,* 23 (Spring 1984): 316–321.
10. Susan E. Brandehoff, "Opinion Survey Shows Untaxed Areas Would Say 'Yes' to Library Levies," *American Libraries,* 17 (December 1986): 859.
11. Bolt, 128.

Recommended Reading

Bonnell, Pamela G. *Fund Raising for the Small Library.* Chicago: American Library Association, 1983.

Howard, Edward N. *Local Power and the Community Library.* Chicago: American Library Association, 1978.

Liebold, Louise Condak. *Fireworks, Brass Bands and Elephants.* Phoenix: Oryx, 1987.

Setterberg, Fred, and Kary Schulman. *Beyond Profit: The Complete Guide to Managing the Nonprofit Organization.* New York: Harper and Row, 1985.

Chapter 4

MIRROR, MIRROR ON THE WALL

The image that a library presents to the community impacts funding, usage of materials, and recruitment of volunteers. *Many factors create image, some obvious and others very subtle.* The community primarily judges the library on the physical building, the behavior of the staff, and the appearance of the collection. Two critical elements in creating the image of the library are the attitude and warmth of the staff. Arrangement of furniture, lighting, attractive displays, and signage also produce a positive impression. The overall appearance of the collection further affects a visitor's opinion. Your library should merchandise reading materials and services since you are "selling" the library to your community.

With few exceptions, the librarian will be primarily responsible for the community's perception of the library. In small communities, no one else is available on a long-term basis who is as visible or as aware of the library's needs. The librarian holds a position in the community which is as potentially important as the position of mayor, superintendent of schools, or chief

The librarian is an important person

of police. Although this recognition is often widely overlooked, it can and should be used to maximum advantage.

Two very diverse reactions toward the library can be identified in almost any community. The first is that people often feel threatened. They do not understand how to use the library, and they are embarrassed at appearing ignorant. While this might be expected of people who have never used a library or who are illiterate, it is also true of college graduates. How many people have told you with a sheepish smile that they used to know the Dewey Decimal system but have now forgotten it? On the other hand, public libraries may generate a reaction of tremendous goodwill from the public. People will support a library for their children or their grandchildren, even if they themselves do not read or use a library. *The library is considered an important asset, and this assessment is widely recognized in the community.* The librarian and the library board sometimes seem to be the only ones who do not acknowledge this vital fact.

Physical Building

EXTERIOR

For a large percentage of the population, the exterior provides the only criterion that people use to judge the library. An unattractive building with peeling paint, unkempt grounds, and sloppy signs will affect usage and funding. *Regardless of how professional the collection or the staff, the community as a whole will remember and judge the library by the face it presents to the world.* The refurbishing of the exterior of the library makes a wonderful project for youth groups, garden clubs, or neighborhood associations.

LAYOUT

The layout of the furniture subtly directs people to specific areas. The major areas of the library should be easily identifiable—adult collections, children's room, reference materials, study areas. Varying ceiling heights and carpet colors can also be used to identify areas.

SIGNS

Colorful, well-kept signs have a surprisingly strong impact. Replacing inappropriate signs or refurbishing necessary ones should be done on a regular schedule. It is far too easy to forget all about the signs once they are finally in place. With few exceptions, hand-lettered signs look hand lettered. A library's appearance can be enhanced by colorful, clean, neatly lettered signs. If you cannot afford printed signs, then buy an inexpensive stencil or rub-off letters. Keep the letters straight and replace the signs frequently. If all else fails, pay to have the work done. Even signs that are covered with contact paper quickly look worn, and the sign that says "Book Return" seems to attract pencil marks, chewing gum, and fingerprints. Other suggestions for lettering and signs are covered in Chapter 6.

INTERIOR

The interior of the library needs to create a welcoming atmosphere. Windows, lighting, displays, the appearance of the collection, and a smile are especially critical elements.

Windows, and thus the ability to see what is going on, attract people from either side of the glass. People driving by can see that the library is appealing and well-used, while people inside benefit from an increased feeling of space and from the natural light. People like natural light, and studies show that it decreases anxiety.

Very few libraries have adequate lighting. This situation does not *have* to exist. While installing a completely new lighting system can be an expensive project, improving existing lighting can be accomplished at a more modest cost. Fluorescent lights are relatively inexpensive, and extra lumens will add immeasurably to the overall atmosphere.

Color plays a major role in how the library is perceived. Research proves that color has the power to motivate one toward a particular action. Red makes one salivate, pink diminishes aggression, and blue leads to relaxation. Freshly painted walls can add immeasurably to the library's appearance. One library recently had a work week in which the carpet was replaced and the walls were repainted by several volunteer organizations.

Merchandising the Collection

Merchandising the collection is a relatively new concept for libraries. The art of retail merchandising can and should be adapted by the community library. *Every technique of retail merchandising in the business world can be applied to the library.* The products that you are selling are the library's services and materials. Unless the product is displayed attractively, it will not reach its greatest potential market.

VISUAL APPEAL

Many merchandising techniques cost little or nothing. The entry area of the library, like the entry area of a retail store, is the prime space for merchandising. The products displayed in the entry area of a store account for a high percentage of all retail sales, which is why a large part of the front of a retail store is dedicated to visually appealing items. When this concept is applied to a library, it forces the librarian to take a hard look at the foyer area. This area is often used inappropriately. The entry area has frequently developed into a sort of stepchild. A large glass display cabinet that fits nowhere else is filled with "rare" books that few ever look at, or the foyer contains furniture that no one ever uses. Floor space needs to be allocated on its ability to generate circulation. Move or discard the unwieldy display cabinets and fill the area with high-interest reading material. Consider adding a bookcase of bestsellers with the front jacket fully displayed.

Many small libraries are visually cluttered. Different types of materials—large-print, foreign language, bestsellers, paperbacks, tapes, records—compete for attention in a small space. It is very difficult to strike a happy balance.

APPEARANCE OF THE COLLECTION

The collection should be colorful and attractive. Careful book selection, particularly of donated material, is very important. Weeding, the bane of all librarians, is critical, not only to keep the collection timely but also for aesthetic reasons. Studies document that weeding will actually increase circulation. Weeding will prove more cost-effective than adding more shelving or space.

Just as "a stitch in time, saves nine," so will mending lengthen the effective life of a book. Books that are not mended on a regular basis will all but disintegrate. Not only will the physical condition of a book affect how it is treated by the reader, but it will also affect how frequently the book will be borrowed.

In small libraries, the majority of people select material because of its physical appearance. Books are merchandised by their covers. Paperbacks and books with jackets will circulate more often than others because of their visual appeal.

ARRANGEMENT OF THE COLLECTION

Studies show that 75 percent of all library material circulates from the second, third, and fourth shelves. For most libraries, that means that one-half of the library is used for storage. How many shelves per section do you have? Would it be better to discard a great many books and display the remainder more effectively? One solution to the inaccessible bottom shelf is to replace it with slanted periodical shelving which can be used for displaying books.

DISPLAYS AND PUBLICITY

Bulletin boards and displays provide other means of merchandising, as do all forms of publicity. News articles, bookmarks, flyers, presentations, programs, and events may be used to promote your library. After years of exposure to high-quality advertising, people expect sophisticated publicity. A poorly printed bookmark or sloppy display will create an immediate impression that the library is not professional. Specific suggestions to improve displays, publicity handouts, and events are covered in Chapters 5 and 6.

Staff

The building, the collection, the displays, and the printed material may create a positive impression, but the key element will always be the staff. Without a friendly, courteous staff, the rest is all but useless. Today, the mood of a store is considered as important as the price, quality, or collection of merchandise. "The quality of one's service is always going to be the predominant factor in determining the success of any operation."[1] The fact that many libraries have survived in spite of thin budgets, inadequate facilities, and a marginal book collection is the direct result of a positive, caring staff.

The librarian creates a friendly and competent atmosphere by his or her attitude and personal philosophy of the library's goals. Business surveys show that an individual's impression of a business is based on interaction with an employee. *If the employee is competent, then the business itself appears to be competent.* This factor alone has incredible ramifications. Since nearly all library users end up at the circulation desk, the attitude and personality of the person working at that desk should be an area of serious concern.

PRIORITIES

Staff, whether paid or volunteer, should be taught that *their number one priority is helping people.* This lesson can be repeated fequently and reinforced by your own example. Any person who enters the library should be greeted, preferably by name, within the first five minutes. In small libraries, if someone asks for help, the staff should stay with the person until he or she has been satisfactorily helped. The library will occasionally be too busy for you or the staff to do this, but most of the time, this is a very realistic goal.

People know each other on a first-name basis in small towns. They are interested in each other. Just pick up a small-town newspaper and you'll not only find out who was born, who got married, and who died in the past week, but you'll also learn who Ed and Alma Hopkins had over for dinner last Sunday night. You have an opportunity to know your clientele very thoroughly through the everyday encounters that occur in that unpredictable process of facing the public.[2]

Everyone knows a horror story about inconsiderate, "superior," or rude staff. Study after study shows that the general public thinks of libraries as forbidding and aloof. People still expect the librarian to enforce silence rigidly. A staff member who reluctantly looks up from a clerical task when asked a question will intimidate most patrons. We spend incredible amounts of energy trying to attract new borrowers, yet we often antagonize the ones we *do* have through poor service. Remember that the people who use the library are already your strongest advocates. These people do not have to be cajoled into visiting the library through events or flyers. They are already there. Treasure them.

Keep in mind that it is difficult for people to ask for help and that many people really do not know how to use the library. Men are supposedly more reluctant to ask questions than women. A strange but true fact is that as they enter a store, men tend to turn left, while women turn right.[3] Careful placement of directional signs can be very helpful.

Library terminology is mysterious to the layperson. "Patron" sounds suspiciously like a wealthy philanthropist of the arts. Consider using "customer" or "user." How many people can distinguish between reference and reserves? Try using the word "information" instead of "reference." Be assured that very few library users know the difference between subject cards and author cards.

APPEARANCE

Just as the exterior of the library needs to have appeal, so does the appearance of the staff. Cartoons often depict librarians as women wearing severe dresses and old-fashioned shoes, hair pulled into a rigid bun. In reality, you will be more likely to have to deal with staff or volunteers who want to wear flip-flops or drink soda at the circulation desk. The librarian should set an example and, within reason, expect the staff to conform.

STAFF INVOLVEMENT

A staff that participates in management decisions will be far more loyal and involved than one that is never consulted. Poeple who work in a

How welcoming is your staff?

given area, whether volunteers or paid staff, often have intelligent, work-saving ideas that can greatly simplify a routine or task. Do not let these wonderful ideas go to waste!

RED TAPE

Sometimes the mechanics of library operation are cumbersome or archaic. Learn to question the rationale behind every form and every step of a given process. While large city libraries need a lengthy application form for new borrowers, smaller libraries may only need the borrower's name, address, zip code, phone number, place of work, and work phone. Why would you need a recommendation or a driver's license?

ATTITUDE

A great deal of attention has been focused on the negative aspects of fines. Certainly all of us are aware of the genuine guilt that most people suffer as they apologetically turn in books that are from a day to a year late. Are people made to feel embarrassment at the circulation desk as they pay fines? Remember that the only people who *have* fines are people who use the library. Give them a big smile and thank them for "supporting their public library."

Overdue notices, damaged books, lost books, and noisy children can be treated in a variety of ways. What attitudes prevail in your library? How is the telephone answered? Do people receive friendly, competent service?

Checklist for Image

Factors as diverse as the physical building, the appearance of the collection, the signage, and the staff's attitude affect the image of the library. Take time to respond to the following checklist. Do not just mentally answer the questions; walk through the library as you make your response. Perhaps a board member or volunteer can also complete the checklist.

THE PHYSICAL BUILDING

> Is it attractive? Appealing?
> Are there windows that allow people to see inside?
> Are the windows clean?
> Are drapes drooping?
> If there are exterior displays, how do they look? How frequently are they changed?
> Are there plants for landscaping?
> Are they trimmed or at least living?
> Do the grounds look well-maintained?
> Is the exterior library sign in good condition?
> What do the mailbox, the book drop, and the flag poles look like?

These are features that everyone in the community sees even if they never use the library. Such factors will form the basis for many people's perceptions of the library.

INTERIOR OF THE LIBRARY

> What is the overall "look" of the library?
> Does it look organized? Clean?
> Are there directional signs, posters, flyers, tax forms, books for sale, donation jars, coupon and pattern exchanges?
> Is it too cluttered?
> Are you satisfied with the color scheme?
> What do the walls look like? Do they need to be repainted?
> Is the carpeting or flooring attractive? Would a professional cleaning help? (Would a local business donate cleaning?)
> Is there enough lighting? Can more lighting be added?
> Is it possible to increase the number or size of the windows?
> Is the furniture attractive? Is the couch losing its insides?
> How deep is the dust?
> Does the wood furniture need to be oiled?
> Can rearrangement of stacks and seating areas give the library a friendlier, more open look?

Does your library have a crisp, clean look?

FOYER

Is it clean?
Is there decrepit furniture? Displays left from Halloween?
Is there a large glass case that is empty or that contains "rare" books?
Does the entry area effectively orient the user to the library?

SIGNS

As you stand in the entry area, what directional signs do you see? (Sometimes signs are unnecessary and only add clutter.)
If you were a new user, what directional signs would you need?
Are the signs appropriate? Is the lettering legible and readable?
Are confusing terms used?
Are the signs crisp and new?
Are they accurate? (Are the 600s really where the sign indicates?)
Is the size of lettering consistent from sign to sign?

THE COLLECTION

Does the shelving look well-maintained? If painted, is it chipped? Are there fingerprints?
Do the shelves sag? (Nothing is as dispiriting as sagging shelves.)
Do the books sit at the edge of the shelf?
Do the books lean?
What part of the collection is on the second, third, and fourth shelves? How much of the collection is on other shelves?

Are the books so crowded that it is difficult to extract one?

Is the collection regularly weeded? Really?

Do books on the shelves need to be mended?

How are the books processed?

Do most books have plastic or paper jackets?

Are the labels at the same level or do they wander up and down?

Are the labels handwritten or typed?

Are the identification stamps neat and straight?

What do the paperbacks look like?

Have the romance books taken over a disproportionate amount of
the library?

Do you treat the paperbacks like stepchildren? (Many people prefer
paperbacks to hardbacks.) Are the racks attractive? Are books
yellowed with curling corners? Should some be discarded?

DISPLAYS AND BULLETIN BOARDS

How do the displays and bulletin boards look?

Are the notices on the bulletin board timely? Attractive? How often
is the bulletin board updated? Weekly? Monthly? Annually?

Are displays filled with books? Are there gaps? Do people actually
take books from the display?

How often are displays restocked?

Where are the displays located?

Are the "prime" locations used effectively?

FLYERS, BOOKMARKS, ETC.

Are bookmarks that list the library's phone number and hours readily available?

Are flyers colorful and appealing?

Do flyers and bookmarks look professional? Is the typing neat? Is
the print clear?

How are the flyers and bookmarks displayed? Are there too many
items on the display table?

THE STAFF

How are the volunteers and staff dressed?

Are they friendly? Do they greet people by name?

Are they obviously willing to help?

Do they just point out the card catalog or do they actually help the
customer find appropriate material?

Are you satisfied that the person at the circulation desk presents the

image and impression by which you want the library to be
   judged?
Is the librarian readily available, or is she or he too busy cataloging,
   mending books, etc.?
Is this a "shhh" library?
Do personnel listen carefully to requests?
How are people with fines and lost books treated?
How does the staff react to children who pull several picture books
   off the shelf? What if the children are noisy?
Do school children receive the same quality of service as adults?
Is the person answering the telephone courteous and helpful?
Does the staff think it is more important to empty the book cart or
   to file cards than to help someone?
Does the staff smile at customers?

Conclusion

If you have been candid, there will be many areas of the library that can
stand improvement. Do not be dismayed. Before any problem can be
solved, it first needs to be recognized. As the image changes, the library
will find that it attracts new users and more volunteers and that staff
morale will improve. Over a period of time, even the powers that be will
recognize the new role of the library; thus funding problems can be dealt
with in a much more positive manner.

Notes

1. Robert S. Alvarez, "From the Editor's Desk," *Library Administrator's
Digest*, 22 (April 1987): 29.
2. Will Manley, "Facing the Public," *Wilson Library Bulletin*, 58 (June 1984):
731.
3. Que Bronson, Books on Display Workshop, Austin, Texas, August 7,
1985.

Recommended Reading

Bronson, Que. *Books on Display*. Washington, D.C.: Metropolitan Washington
   Library Council, 1982.

Chapter 5

SPREADING THE WORD

In most small libraries, responsibility for effective public relations rests squarely on the shoulders of the librarian. However, the importance of public relations is rarely understood. The essence of public relations is communication. Publicity increases use of services, attendance at programs, and awareness of the library. Publicity impacts funding and allows the library to express its needs. The direct correlation between publicity and community awareness can not be overemphasized. The presentation of a wonderful program is worthless without an audience; the selection of outstanding materials is wasted if no one checks them out; and professional, courteous service is useless if there is no one at whom to smile. Used effectively, publicity increases budgets and generates donations. It can create new awareness of the library or serve as a reminder of its existence. Publicity helps the library to express its needs for better funding, more volunteers, or new equipment. The assumption that the public or government officials are aware of funding problems is simply not valid. Remember the squeaky wheel. . . .

Director of public relations

Basic Considerations

A tremendous variety of potential sources exists for publicizing the library. These can be as varied as newspaper articles, overdues, letters of appreciation, or presentations to local groups. Learn to work closely with key people and recognize the unique value of each publicity source.

There must be a *plan* for developing community relations and increasing public awareness. *It is critical that the plan be written, discussed, reviewed, and then put into action.* "There is so much that can be done, so much that doubtless ought to be done, that rigorous selection of tasks and priorities must precede the start of the execution. All options and possibilities must be examined in the light of payoff."[1]

> There is evidence of increasing interest on the part of librarians in learning how to use the tools of promotion, but very little evidence that this knowledge is put to use with a purposeful and measurable end result firmly in mind. It's a bit like taking a short course in how to handle a hammer, nails, and a saw, and then proceeding to use them without a blueprint or pattern. You could even build a good dog house without a blueprint, but it would certainly be wiser first to determine (a) if you have a dog, (b) if or why you need a house for the dog, (c) whether the dog can be taught to use it when built, and (d) the actual size of the dog for whom it is intended.[2]

The librarian, the staff, the volunteers, and the board need pride in the publicity that is created. Any material that leaves the library should be well-presented, accurate, and attractive. Avoid sloppy, poorly printed materials. The quality of work makes a definite statement about the library's image. "Remember that you're competing with every Madison Avenue ad agency. Do it well."[3]

All publicity needs to be created in terms of the *users*. Articles and presentations need to be worded to reflect what the library will do for *them*. Tell the potential donor or user how their involvement or support will benefit them, whether the topic is volunteers (get to know your neighbors), donations (tax deduction, goodwill) or governmental funding (voter approval). Never assume that people are already aware of the benefits.

The headline, or "grabber," is often the most important part of any form of publicity. The real value of a newspaper column entitled "The Library Shelf" is as a reminder that the library exists. Many people skim a flyer or the newspaper—be sure that an awareness of the library is created, even if the material is read casually. The same rationale applies to photographs.

It is not necessary to be original. Large libraries churn out publicity

Newspaper:
(Organizations,
etc.)   _____

Address: _____

Deadline: _____

Contact: _____

Phone: _____

Date Compiled: _____

Fig. 9.   Information sheet for news outlets

that can be readily adapted for your use. Keep a file of ideas or flyers that appeal to you. Reuse material that deals with annual events after a year or two and change it slightly. The American Library Association and your state library issue publicity releases just for libraries to copy.

If at all possible, budget for public relations. A rule of thumb is to allow 1–2 percent of the total budget for public relations. Printing costs, paper, supplies, and mailing expenses are just a few of the valid budget items. A line item in the budget acknowledges the necessity and importance of public relations.

The library cannot create too much publicity. This statement should be engraved on the librarian's desk. After the library had contributed weekly articles to the local newspaper for two years, a long-term volunteer commented that two of her friends had never heard of the library and had suggested that the library put an article in the local paper! A recent article from the advertising industry indicated that an advertisement has to appear ten times before it is noticed, let alone read. When it is read, 60 percent of the readers forget the content within twenty-four hours.[4]

Someone—you or a volunteer—needs to prepare an information sheet on each of the news sources (figure 9). Include the name of the news outlet (whether television, radio, news article, or organization), address, deadline, contact, and phone number, as well as any stray facts. Many irritating problems will be eliminated if the format that the organization prefers is identified. Note the date that the information was compiled and update the list periodically.

An enormous variety of potential outlets for publicity exists even in very small communities. News articles, group presentations, radio and television, handouts, mailouts, book sales, and even overdues can and should be utilized. Make your own additions to the following list.

Newspapers
Newsletters
  School
  Church
  Club
  Business
  Neighborhood
Radio
Television
Community Events
  Carnival
  Pancake breakfast
  Rodeo
Flyers
  Grocery stores
  School children
  School faculty
  Library

Chamber of Commerce
Better Business Bureau
School administration office
Presentations
  Organizations
  Clubs
  Back-to-school night at schools
Mailouts
  Bank statements—inserts
  Friends of the library meeting
  Fundraising letter
  Overdues
  Thank you notes
  Bookmarks
Activities
  Book sales
  Programs
  Storytime

News Articles

Newspapers provide a time-honored yet very effective way for libraries to communicate with the public. Certainly the most common outlet is news articles. Responsibility for the articles can be assigned to a volunteer—not necessarily one who works in the library. Appeal to former newspaper people or aspiring writers. This appeal would even make a good news article. If you cannot find a writer, at least find a volunteer who will remind you of the need to write an article.

If a large part of your population speaks another language or is functionally illiterate, the written media may be useless. Alternatives are visual or verbal messages, which can be provided by radio, television, or photographs. Use of fotonovelas (see page 32) has proved very effective in reaching the Spanish population. Be sure to include articles in any foreign-language newspaper that is published in your area.

DEADLINES

It is difficult to be timely in preparing news articles. Many newspapers require a lead time of two to two and a half weeks. Establish a pattern for news releases and then follow it. Prepare a schedule of yearly events. Include library programs, potential topics by season (taxes, wildflowers), holidays, and the summer reading program. The sheet will help identify potential topics for news releases and will also help the library organize its publicity schedule. Nothing falls through the cracks as readily as publicity.

EDITORS

Before asking for permission to write a weekly newspaper article, you may want to take the editor to lunch. At the very least, introduce yourself and give him or her a library card and a handout about the library. Editors tend to be strong advocates of the public library. They are usually also committed to improving the quality of life in the community. Involve the editor in your concerns about the library. Ask for ideas to increase usage, reach new people, and involve the community. Editors can provide valuable insights into the local community. You can only benefit by tapping this resource.

During a recent library public relations workshop, a pitch had been made for involving the local newspaper editor in promoting the library. The group was discussing the various weights of paper when the editor walked in to cover the event for his newspaper. Within minutes, he was talking about bond paper, weight considerations, and cost factors and quickly became very much a part of the workshop. Think of the advantages of having that editor actively involved as an outspoken advocate for the library!

PHOTOGRAPHS

Given a choice between a written article and a photograph, always choose the photograph. A picture really *is* worth a thousand words. Photographs can be understood by everyone, including nonreaders and young children. People recognize friends and identify them with the library. An older person reading to a child delivers a wonderful message. If a photograph is included with a news release, add the phrase "with picture" to the article. Use rubber cement to attach the photograph to a separate sheet with the caption written below the picture. Do not expect to have the picture returned. Do not put the caption on the back of the photo. Editors are easily antagonized by pictures of unidentified or incorrectly identified people.

Community newspapers are not the only potential target for articles. Schools often have a newspaper, as do clubs and organizations. Neighborhoods, business organizations (realtors, banks), and churches sometimes publish a newsletter. The school district may send out a monthly or annual newsletter. Many of these editors would be delighted to have an article or picture about the library to include in their publication.

FORMAT

Use of the following form will assure that the basic data is covered. This information should appear at the top of any article submitted for publication.

To:	(Include name, section of paper, title if regular column)
For Release:	(Date article is to appear—might be "as soon as possible")
From:	(Include name of library, contact person, phone number)
Article:	(Double space on one side of paper only)

Try to limit the article to one and a half pages. At the bottom of the first page, write " - More - ". At the top of the second page, write " - Add One - ". Do not break a paragraph from page to page. At the end of the article, write " - End -".

News articles, no matter what the topic, need to include certain elements. Many people never read further than the first line of the article, so be sure that the key points are made immediately. The article must state *who, what, where, when, and how,* preferably in the first sentence. Most of us know this very basic fact, yet we fail to reread the article just to be certain that the important elements have been included. It is embarrassing to read an article that *you* wrote in which a key element, such as the date of the new library program, is missing.

Avoid overstatements filled with adjectives, such as, "the world-renowned author of numerous prestigious books . . . ." News articles should be as concise and factual as possible. Use short paragraphs, double-space the article, and use only one side of the page. Try to use humor or a catchy first line. Avoid library jargon. Editors will welcome straightforward, factual articles, and they will smile when they see you coming.

TOPICS

The library is a busy place, and the topics covered should reflect this diversity. In the confusion of day-to-day life, it is easy to forget news that should be featured. Publicity should cover not only resources and available materials but also library objectives, problems, accomplishments, and projects. Potential topics which might be included in news releases are listed below.

> *Volunteers*—new, old, sign painter, shelving assembler, groups, window washer, storyteller, board member(s), maybe even the Monday volunteers
> *Gifts*—donations of money, stocks, books, memorial donations, equipment, donations of services (CPA, architecture)
> *Personnel*—new and old employees
> *Timely topics*—holidays, skiing, scholarships, gardening, summer sports, annual report
> *Activities*—presentations, events, meetings, programs

Materials—films, tapes, cameras, mystery books, biographies, magazines
Services—storytime, reference, reader's advice
Changes—hours of operation, location, fees for services

Television and Radio

Most television and radio stations set aside a designated amount of time for public service announcements. Many stations will welcome news releases from the library. The first step is to contact the station and meet the people with whom you will deal. Public service announcements last either twenty seconds (forty-five to fifty words), thirty seconds (sixty-five words), or sixty seconds (125–50 words). Identify both the format the station prefers and the audience that the station will reach. Radio and television provide an excellent way to reach people who do not read the newspaper or are functionally illiterate. Besides using the public service announcement, the station may publicize your message through call-in shows, news programs, editorial replies, bulletin boards, daily calendars, and interviews. Involve the station's newscasters. Give them library cards. Ask for their ideas. Take them a plate of cookies to thank them for their help. When a person is involved, he or she becomes an advocate for the library.

Involve the media!

The American Library Association and many state library organizations provide spot announcements that can be readily adapted for your community. Emphasis is usually on National Library Week, the summer reading program or topics of current interest, such as illiteracy. Book sales and events might be highlighted, as can the availability of tax forms. Some of the larger libraries now offer weekly shows that feature interviews with authors or that present book reviews. The Beverly Hills

Public Library offers their program "In Print" to libraries and to municipal, educational, and library cable channels at no cost.[5] Sources for the materials mentioned here are:

American Library Association, Public Information Office, 50 E. Huron St., Chicago, IL 60611, (312) 944-6780 (posters, bookmarks, publicity items for National Library Week)

Beverly Hills Public Library, 444 N. Rexford, Beverly Hills, CA 90210, (213) 550-4721

Children's Book Council, 175 Fifth Ave., New York, NY 10010, (212) 254-2666 (Children's Book Week and summer reading program materials)

The format and criteria for the public service announcements should be similar to that used for news articles. Many stations accept postcards with a typed public service announcement; this is a quick, simple solution to verbal publicity. Address this announcement: Attn., Public Service Announcement Department.

The library will occasionally be the feature for a television or radio story. The person who represents the library should not only be very knowledgeable but should also be capable of presenting the case in a positive manner. A meandering presentation of obvious ignorance has a poor effect on the library image. Most newscasters will gladly share their intended questions *before* the camera starts to roll, but only if you ask.

Unfortunately, special coverage is often associated with controversy, such as a censorship issue. If the material is at all controversial, be well informed before the interview begins. If the topic deals with a censorship case, try to avoid specifics and discuss the long-term effects of censorship rather than justification of a particular title. A discussion of banned books throughout history can lighten the atmosphere. The following list represents just a few of the many books banned over the years in the United States.

The American Heritage Dictionary of the English Language.
Blume, Judy, *Deenie.*
Burgess, Anthony. *A Clockwork Orange.*
Cormier, Robert. *The Chocolate War.*
Huxley, Aldous. *Brave New World.*
Kesey, Ken. *One Flew over the Cuckoo's Nest.*
Salinger, J. D. *The Catcher in the Rye.*
Shakespeare, William. *The Merchant of Venice.*
Steig, William. *Sylvester and the Magic Pebble.*
Steinbeck, John. *The Grapes of Wrath.*
Zindel, Paul. *My Darling, My Hamburger.*[6]

For a more complete list of banned books and exhibit materials as well as information about professional support in a censorship controversy, contact the American Library Association, Office for Intellectual Freedom, 50 E. Huron St., Chicago, IL 60611.

When a news feature covers library funding topics such as potential library budget cuts or a bond issue, be prepared to justify the funding in a way that appeals to a broad range of people. Tell the audience how budget cuts will affect *them*. Further discussion about funding and the political process are discussed in Chapter 3.

Presentations

Any time a group of people gathers, an opportunity exists to promote the library. Most towns have so many groups, clubs, organizations, and associations that at first glance the job seems overwhelming. Actually, after a *second* look, the job may still seem overwhelming.

It helps to realize that *you* do not have to make the presentations. The volunteer who makes presentations for your library does not necessarily need to work in the library. The person should enjoy talking to groups and like the visibility she or he receives. On the other hand, you will have to coordinate any presentations that are made. The library can contact various organizations to see if they are interested in a future program. A volunteer can do this just as effectively as you can. The presentation can last five minutes or thirty minutes depending on the group's needs.

The most effective presentation seems to be a combination of a personable speaker, an attractive poster with pictures of the library, and a box of books that will appeal to the audience. Library cards can be issued, and books can be checked out at the end of the talk. Hand out a flyer or bookmark and perhaps a membership application to the Friends group.

Many service clubs contribute to nonprofit organizations. Be sure to let these people know that the library has financial needs. Give them a choice of how they can support the library. Perhaps they will participate in an annual event, help fund a new copying machine, or even make an annual pledge to the library. Some organizations will do all three, but *only if they are asked*. Chapters 1 and 2 include more information about organizations and their importance to the library.

Parents at back-to-school nights and teachers at the local schools are important groups to talk to. Each year, make a five-minute presentation at each of the schools to all the parents. Tell them that you provide a secondary library resource for their children, that you offer free library service, and that you have materials for their children as well as for them.

In early fall, have a retired teacher make a short presentation to the faculty of each school. Hand out flyers that reiterate the key points (figure 10) and bookmarks with the library hours that can be posted on the class bulletin board. Unfortunately, a community library that works

THE WESTBANK COMMUNITY LIBRARY

WHO: Free library cards for anyone

WHERE: Second Floor, Texas Commerce Bank
            2224 Walsh Tarlton
            327-3045

WHEN: Monday–Thursday 10–6
            Friday 10–4
            Saturday (1st & 3rd) 10–1

WHY: The WCL serves as a secondary library resource for
            the Eanes Independent School District as well as a
            source of recreational reading for the entire communi-
            ty. Selective purchase of material over the past year
            has added books on World War II and science experi-
            ments, and five sets of literary criticism. The majority
            of the 17,000-book collection, including six sets of
            encyclopedias and back issues of magazines, may be
            checked out.

We are always glad to assist your students by putting books on
reserve for major assignments. This will only work, however, if we
are notified before all the books are checked out. Call the library, or
use the attached form to keep us informed of major assignments. As
the community library, we want very much to serve everyone as
effectively as possible. If you have suggestions for specific titles or
ideas for better service, I am always interested in hearing from you.
A special thanks to all of you who have made our library such a
success.

Beth Fox—Librarian—327-3045

The form attached had these column headings:

Assignment   *Probable Dates*   *Number of Students*   *Grade*

Fig. 10.   Information flyer for teachers

closely with the local school district is the exception rather than the rule.
The close ties that you create with the school district will reap many
unexpected benefits. In one area during the past year, *every school* origi-
nated and orchestrated a fundraiser to benefit their community library.
Response to the flyer in terms of notification of assignments will be slow.
At the Westbank Community Library, the third attempt produced only

Dear Teacher: Date:_____

_____ came to the library today. We

regret that we are unable to fill the request for _____

_____ because:

_____ All materials on this subject are in use (checked out).

_____ Reasonable search failed to supply suitable materials.

_____ All material on this subject is reference and must be used in
       the library.

_____ Further clarification of question is needed.

_____ Other/Notes _____

       _____

       _____

Telephone: _____

                              _____, Librarian

Fig. 11.   Letter to teachers

eight returns from 350 flyers. On the other hand, teachers do call about
large assignments. They are certainly more aware of our existence and
our concern. On a daily basis, students now show up with a sentence that
begins, "My teacher said. . . ." Another library used the letter shown in
figure 11, with very positive results, as a follow-up after children had
checked out all available resources.

Flyers

Successful use of flyers depends on appeal and widespread distribution.
Sources for *free* distribution are limited only by your imagination. Be

creative. Recently the Lake Travis (Texas) Friends Organization began to distribute a newsletter by enclosing it with bank statements. The bank considers the mailing costs a public service. Grocery stores will usually include a flyer in the bag of each customer. The manager can give you an estimate of the number needed. Schools, with advance permission from the superintendent, will allow you to promote programs as diverse as the summer reading club, Junior Great Books, and fundraising events. Don't forget the packet of information the superintendent's office hands out to parents of new students. Flyers should be available at the Better Business Bureau and the Chamber of Commerce. They can be included in the newspaper as part of a page or as a separate insert. The local paper may let you insert a flyer at no cost if the library provides the labor. A group of six women recently inserted 6,000 flyers into the local paper while chatting happily.

Bookmarks are such a standard library promotional piece that it is easy to overlook their presence. Bookmarks are a form of flyer. They provide a handy reference guide for hours, location, and storytime dates. Bookmarks can be used as a mini-newspaper for library news. The information on the bookmark can readily be changed to include new information or to update old. For years, the bookmark has served as a subject bibliography or a means to promote library services. (See figure 12.) It is a very inexpensive, effective device.

All flyers need to be attractive and appealing. Colorful paper, a variety of print styles, and layout will affect the number of people who pause to glance at the material. (See Chapter 6.) Flyers should be simple, and words should be kept to a minimum. *The message should be clear.* (See figure 13.)

Community Events

Awareness of the library can be created through community events. Besides the programs, book fairs, or art shows that the library sponsors, there exists a whole range of other activities. Suggestions for evaluating the fundraising aspects of community events are detailed in Chapter 3. Carnivals, Founder's Day parades, talent shows, Fourth of July celebrations, or similar events take place in your community. Select a few key events and be sure that the library, or better yet, the Friends group, sponsors a booth and is a visible part of the event.

Display attractive books, brochures about the library, photographs of activities, a scrapbook, membership applications for the Friends group, and the ever-present bookmark. Include a poster of Polaroid pictures of all your volunteers labeled, "Do you know these wonderful volunteers?" (Don't forget to include the library board.) Be brave—go ahead and issue library cards and even check out the books. Decorate the booth with twenty helium balloons and bright colors. Then staff it with people who *smile.*

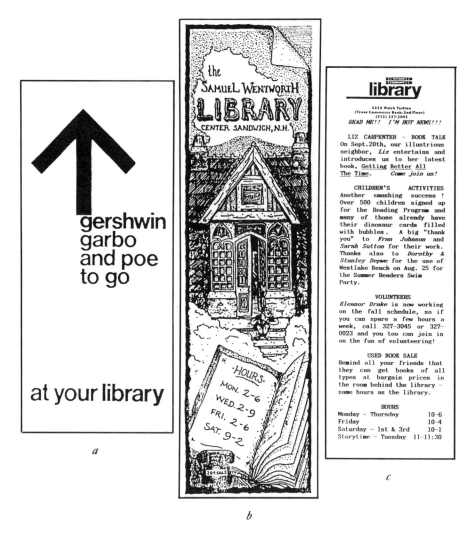

a

b

library

2224 Walsh Tarlton
(Texas Commerce Bank-2nd Floor)
(512) 327-3045
READ ME!! I'M HOT NEWS!!!

LIZ CARPENTER - BOOK TALK
On Sept.20th, our illustrious
neighbor, *Liz* entertains and
introduces us to her latest
book, Getting Better All
The Time.   *Come join us!*

CHILDREN'S   ACTIVITIES
Another smashing success !
Over 500 children signed up
for the Reading Program and
many of those already have
their dinosaur cards filled
with bubbles . A big "thank
you" to *Fran Johnson* and
Sarah Sutton for their work.
Thanks also to *Dorothy &
Stanley Depew* for the use of
Westlake Beach on Aug. 25 for
the Summer Readers Swim
Party.

VOLUNTEERS
Eleanor Drake is now working
on the fall schedule, so if
you can spare a few hours a
week, call 327-3045 or 327-
0023 and you too can join in
on the fun of volunteering!

USED BOOK SALE
Remind all your friends that
they can get books of all
types at bargain prices in
the room behind the library -
same hours as the library.

HOURS
Monday - Thursday   10-6
Friday   10-4
Saturday - 1st & 3rd   10-1
Storytime - Tuesday   11-11:30

c

Fig. 12. Bookmarks can provide all kinds of information; (a) American Library Association, (b) Samuel Wentworth Library, Center Sandwich, New Hampshire, (c) Westbank Community Library, Austin, Texas

Mailouts

Every mailout becomes a piece of publicity—even reminders for board meetings. Most meetings that are directed at a specific group will require a mailing—the Friends, the board, the advisory council. Some forms of fundraising can only be handled by mail. Direct mail solicitation has proved effective for many organizations. Overdues certainly deliver a

USED BOOK SALE
Thousands of Books
Paperback • Hardback • Fiction • Non-Fiction

Sponsored by the

Friends of the Westbank
Community Library

Where: Texas Commerce Bank
2224 Walsh Tarlton
2nd Floor at Library
(across from Barton Square)
Phone: 327-3045

When: Hours same as Library
Mon.-Thur. — 10-6
Fri. — 10-4
1st & 3rd Sat. — 10-1

Why: Books are a terrific bargain
at 25ᶜ-$1.00.
Support Your Library

Book Donations Welcome
Tax Deductible — Receipts Available

•Romance•Classics•Mysteries•Childrens•Cookbooks•Textbooks•Biographies•

Fig. 13. The flyer should convey a clear message

message. Remember that the only people who have overdue books are library users—those elusive human beings you've searched for.

With the cost of postage, the expense of any mailout becomes an important factor. This does not mean that you should not use mailouts as a very effective form of publicity; it only means that you should use them

Fig. 14. Informational postcard

with caution. Libraries are eligible for bulk postage rates. However, there is an annual fee, and very specific guidelines must be followed for each mailout. If you ever find a volunteer who understands all the criteria, treasure this person. He or she is worth solid gold. Currently, the annual fee is fifty dollars, so several mailouts would need to be planned during the year to justify the cost. Also, each mailout must consist of 200 or more pieces of identical mail. Even changing the envelope can cause a problem. Bulk rate *cannot* be used for bills, such as overdue notices.

Concerned about the lack of contact between the library and the members of the Friends group, one library sends postcards quarterly to all members. The postcards contain a potpourri of information about the library, such as upcoming library programs, election dates for new officers, scheduled book talks, and seasonal information. (See figure 14.) Letters to acknowledge memorial donations are also a form of publicity. These donations should be handled carefully. *Never* notify the family of the deceased of the amount of the donation. Acknowledgment needs to be made to the donor as well as to the family of the deceased.

Thank-you letters serve as a very effective form of publicity. Letters should be written to anyone who has made a significant contribution. This includes the teenager who donated his time as a lifeguard at the summer reading program party. Thank the calligrapher who letters your signs, the woman who writes the newspaper articles, and the program chairman for the Friends organization. Always write to people who donate money and occasionally to people who donate books. Thank-you letters recognize people who already care about the library. It is easy to overlook a long-term volunteer in the confusion of day-to-day life. The board secretary will often take responsibility for writing letters. If not, find a volunteer who will at least help.

If a form letter is used, it must either clearly be a form letter (figure 15), or it must not look at all like a form letter. People are antagonized if they think you have "tricked" them with a form letter. The form letter can be personalized by a handwritten thank-you or a quick note at the bottom of the page.

Thank you for your donation to the _____ Library. Each contribution is important to the success of our library.

Community energy and enthusiasm created a library for our area. Your tax deductible gift assures that our dream of a permanent building becomes a reality. Together, we will build a library of which we can all be proud.

Name of donor(s): _____

Amount: _____ Date received: _____

Fig. 15. Sample thank-you letter to be used with library letterhead

Activities

Specific activities that the library sponsors also publicize the library. The activities are probably promoted through traditional forms of publicity, but the event itself creates further awareness. Common events are library programs and book sales. Two people chatting in the grocery line about the storytime or the upcoming book fair generate positive publicity. The overheard comment, "My child loves storytime," has tremendous impact. This casual remark is probably worth more than hundreds of flyers. Events cause people to talk about the library and allow them to participate. Once they have participated, no matter how casually, subtle ties are created. A person who bakes a cake for the cakewalk or donates helium for balloons has affirmed his or her support of the library. Over a period of time, these ties become identified with "my library."

Book Bags, T-Shirts

Publicity and awareness can be created through a book bag or other item that carries a message about the library. A number of vendors sell pre-printed promotional material. Hats, visors, t-shirts, buttons, rubber stamps, bumper stickers, and pennants can be purchased. Promotional materials can be used as fundraisers, as prizes in library events, or as a thank-you for donations of time or money. The item thus gives double service to the library. First, it carries an advertising visual message, and second, it becomes a desirable item.

A library will occasionally create individualized items. Be aware that personalized items cannot be returned. Problems can arise when deciding how many t-shirts with the library logo to purchase and what sizes will actually sell. It is almost guaranteed that if you order large shirts, only small people will buy them. The cost of all unsold items will have to be deducted from any profit. Whether the item is customized or not, never hesitate to point out that the library is a poor nonprofit organization which would greatly appreciate a reduction in price. *It is all right to ask for special discounts.*

Logo on book bag for building campaign

Displays and Bulletin Boards

Bulletin boards allow the library to promote special programs, indicate the hours of operation, and display lists of books. They can also be used to promote area events, thus becoming an important information resource.

Displays can be used to advertise materials that are available in the library. These displays should be simple, not only because you do not have time to create anything else, but also because people are leery of disturbing elaborate displays. The topic needs to be broad enough that replacement material can be found readily by the staff. If general topics, such as gardening or travel, are used almost any library can keep the display well-stocked. Many times, a descriptive sign is not necessary. If one is used, however, keep the graphics very simple and use no more than three words.

Displays can be as simple as a shelf of bestsellers, a rack of attractive nonfiction in a prime location, or a stack of former bestsellers on the circulation desk. The bookrack in the entry to the Westbank Community Library holds twenty-four books. It is kept stocked with attractive non-fiction hardbacks, and at least six books need to be replaced on a *quiet* day. Even if people do not check the material out, they will be more aware of the diversity of the collection.

Empty buildings provide a potential source for large displays. Prime window space that many people walk past makes an ideal location for colorful, large displays that can be tied into material available in the library.

Merchandising space exists at the end of the bookstacks and at the circulation desk. Take a hard look at the grocery store. The checkout counter and the ends of the aisles are considered prime areas for spur-of-the-moment purchases and are therefore crowded with a last-minute choice of items. The circulation desk is a very powerful merchandising area, both because there is a built-in delay at this point and because it is an area of high usage.

Book "dumps," cardboard boxes like bookstores use to hold paperbacks, can increase circulation dramatically at the circulation desk. End panels *can* be used for things other than posters. Remember that every aspect of retail merchandising will work in your library.

Conclusion

The need for effective public relations cannot be overemphasized. Somewhere in the busy life of the librarian, time must be set aside to at least *coordinate* a public relations program. This program will reinforce the library's value to the community, increase use of the library, and ensure attendance at programs. Publicity will draw attention to the library's needs and will ultimately affect funding. Having identified topics and potential sources, the author will discuss the mechanics of creation in the next chapter.

Notes

1. Carlton Rochell, *Wheeler and Goldhor's Practical Administration of Public Libraries*, rev. ed. (New York: Harper and Row, 1981), 275.

2. Marian S. Edsall, *Library Promotion Handbook* (Phoenix: Oryx, 1980), 9.

3. Virginia Baeckler and Linda Larson, *GO, PEP, and POP!* (New York: The Unabashed Librarian, 1976), 16.

4. Robert S. Alvarez, "Impact! Community Awareness Project," *Library Administrator's Digest*, 20 (May 1985): 72.

5. Michael Cart, "Lights, Camera, Hyperventilate!" *Library Journal*, 111 (May 1, 1986): 89–91.

6. American Library Association, Office for Intellectual Freedom, *Banned Books Exhibit* (Chicago: ALA), 1–3.

Recommended Reading

Bronson, Que. *Books on Display*. Washington, D.C.: Metropolitan Washington Council of Governments, 1982.

Edsall, Marian S. *Library Promotion Handbook*. Phoenix: Oryx, 1980.

Rossie, Charles M., Jr. *Media Resource Guide: How to Tell Your Story*. 4th ed. Los Angeles: Foundation for American Communications, 1985.

Chapter 6

CUT AND PASTE

Every person that you reach, whether through a verbal, visual, or written message, becomes more aware of the library. Each of these persons either is or will be a taxpayer. This fact alone has tremendous ramifications. Appropriate selection of topics, widespread distribution, and the quality of presentation will determine a library's public relations success. Graphic presentation creates a problem for many librarians because they have little knowledge of basic concepts of layout or choices of materials. Reproduction, layout, and paper selection determine the quality of the presentation. *The appeal of the actual presentation will become part of the image by which the community judges the library.*

Pride

The key to the quality of presentation is pride. People make judgments about an organization based on any material that is distributed. That is why companies spend millions of dollars on advertising campaigns and

Pride is the key

willingly underwrite high-expense items like color brochures. A poorly written, misspelled, sloppily printed flyer sends a very clear message—even if it is the wrong message. Take a hard look at your bookmarks and flyers and see what the actual message is. Pride in any material that carries the library logo will go a long way to ensure the correct message.

Equipment

As in any job, having the right equipment can greatly simplify the work. A typewriter that creates a sharp, clean image will certainly make your job a lot easier. With luck, you will have a self-correcting typewriter or a good printer with a word processor. If you do not, a quality typewriter should be a high-priority budget item.

Many typewriters and computers can print in different sizes of type as well as in different type styles. Use of various styles and sizes of type give interest to the text and highlight key points. The desirability—even the necessity—of creating a crisp, clear copy cannot be overemphasized.

Another very desirable piece of equipment is a copy machine. Life is much easier when such a machine is located in the library or, at least, the library has ready access to one. The copier is not only incredibly useful to the librarian, but it is also useful to the community. Cost justification should be the problem in obtaining a copier, not justification of usefulness. Publicize the need for a machine in terms of a tax write-off for a local business and promise community recognition for the donation. Copy machines have a very low replacement value. Ask a local copy machine dealer if he or she will help you find a donor. One library received two machines as a result of one newspaper article. Assuming you get a copier, ask the copy machine dealer to donate the service contract. Sometimes a local business, the local newspaper, or the mayor's office will let you use their machine at no cost if you provide the paper.

A copy machine allows you to manipulate the text. Paragraphs can be cut out and reinserted at another point. Enlarging or reducing an item often affects its appeal. (See figure 16.) Appropriate art work can be attached to the text, and special borders or letters can be adapted to fit the layout.

Printing Versus Photocopying

Print shops used to be the only option for quality multicopy reproductions. Widespread availability of copy machines has changed this. If a quality copier is available at no charge, it should be used. Even if the work has to be paid for, a copier will be cheaper than printing unless you are making hundreds of copies. In any case, always ask for the work to be donated or at least discounted. If the work is done for free, the printer will often request that an acknowledgment of his business be made on the flyer.

Ask the printer for help. Can this be done more inexpensively? How would you improve the text, the layout, and the margins? After all, the printer is an expert. Many customers are embarrassed to ask questions, yet doing so can make a tremendous difference in the total cost and quality of the work. Furthermore, you have just involved another person as a new library advocate.

Traditionally, work done by a printer has been typeset. Typesetting costs are determined by the required number of letters. For most library purposes, a carbon ribbon typewriter will produce letters that copy just as effectively as if they had been typeset. Typesetting is rarely necessary or even desirable for library materials.

If the work is to be cut to exact requirements, it will be necessary to leave adequate margins on photocopied material or to have the work printed so that it is aligned exactly on each page. A good example is borrower cards, which by necessity have very small margins.

A copy shop or a printer will always ask you to "proof" the work before final reproduction. *Always read the material twice.* On a very expensive gala invitation, the Westbank Library ended up as the Wetbank Library. If the work was done incorrectly and the error was not your fault, refuse to accept the finished product and insist that it be redone. Allow adequate lead time to get the work done. If the piece is to be mailed out Wednesday, ask for the completed work the previous Friday. Strange delays often occur with deadlines and printed material.

"Camera ready" is printers' jargon for copy that is ready to be reproduced as it is. *Camera ready* means that the art work and the typing can be reproduced to make clean, crisp copy. This service can be provided by the copy shop or the printer, but you will pay more for it. Sometimes the extra cost can be justified but it should not be necessary for inexpensive flyers.

Print or copy shops often have an industrial paper cutter that cuts through reams of paper with a single stroke. Whenever you are cutting large quantities of paper, remember this—even for material that you produced in-house. Although the shop may charge you for the service, it will probably not cost more than a dollar a cut—an excellent bargain.

Layout

The material should usually cover *one* concept. The wording on a flyer needs to be as simple as possible. Editing material to eliminate extra words will always add to the overall appeal. Wide margins give visual appeal and help focus attention on the message.

Fig. 16. Same flyer, two different effects

LETTERING

A rule of thumb is to use different print styles to create interest, but limit the type to two different lettering styles. Typeface falls into five main categories—roman, gothic block, text, italic, and script. Some typefaces are very difficult to read. Plain block lettering (Helvetica Medium) is the easiest to read. In general, lower case lettering is more readable. Type without serifs will increase the professional look of the material. (See figure 17.) Remember that the quality of type can affect the number of people who will actually read the item.

The distance and width between letters will also affect legibility. (See figure 18.) For signs, letters should be large enough to be easily readable —two or three times larger than necessary. The contrast between background color and letters affects readability. The most visible combinations are black on yellow, black on white, and yellow on black.

If your typewriter or computer printer does not have different type fonts, purchase some inexpensive rub-off letters to highlight the text. Rub-off letters and stencils are available through office supply stores.

Fig. 16 (*cont.*). Same flyer, two different effects

Fig. 17. Type style comparison guide

Universe No. 49

Universe No.55

Universe No.57

Univers No.59

Univers No.65

Univers No.67

Univers No.75

Fig. 18. Width of letters

PASTEUP

The original layout needs to be done on white paper, so that the material will copy without shadows. Any corrections can be made with correction fluid. Layout sheets with blue graph lines can be purchased but are necessary only for very accurate work. Use a T square and a ruler to align material on the original layout.

Pencils can be purchased with blue lead that will not reproduce on a copy machine. They can be very useful for making the actual layout. Each time material, particularly pictures, is reproduced, it loses a little density. If you are making four bookmarks to a sheet, it is best to create four originals and then paste them on to one sheet for the final copy. (See figure 19.) When a picture or type reproduces too lightly, use a fine-tip felt pen to darken the appropriate areas.

Rubber cement (an adhesive that allows you to remove an item or relocate it) should be used to attach the various components to the layout sheet. For easiest removal, the rubber cement should be applied to the layout sheet and to the item that you are adding. Excess adhesive can be removed by rubbing gently with your finger. It is possible that you may have art work, text, and special rub-off letters attached to the layout sheet. (This is definitely a cut-and-paste project.)

If shadows appear on the copy, use correction fluid, also called liquid paper or whiteout, to clean up the copy and remove lines, shadows, and dots. (It's hard to believe, but many librarians don't know about this blood pressure–reducing product.) At this point the original may look terrible, but it can still make excellent copies.

Fig. 19. Four bookmarks arranged for easy printing

Artwork

Artwork may come from a number of sources. Inexpensive booklets that contain artwork for various topics can be purchased from bookstores and office supply stores. These books contain drawings, special lettering, and borders. The artwork is called "clip art" because it can be clipped and reused. The American Library Association also publishes a book of clip art just for libraries (figure 20). If your state library has a library development collection, it probably has useful material that you can borrow. Artwork can also be reproduced from books that are no longer under copyright. Many newspapers subscribe to "mat services" for ready-to-use art. Your local editor may occasionally be willing to share material.

Inexpensive graphics programs can be purchased for microcomputers. These programs provide lettering, borders, and artwork. Other sources of artwork include children's books, piano books, and newspapers, which often contain pen and ink drawings. Artwork or special lettering can be done by individuals in the community—perhaps even by a student. Don't forget the art teacher as a source.

Fig. 20. Examples of library-oriented clip art

Logo

Logos are an important tool in merchandising. They provide immediate identification of material from a particular industry or source. Learn to use the library logo effectively on book bags, posters, stationery, envelopes, newsletters, annual reports, and mailing labels. Select a logo that is contemporary and that enhances the library's image. Choose a graphic that can be reduced or enlarged as needed, as you will want to use the logo on all types of material. (See figure 21 for examples.)

Fig. 21. Select a logo to enhance the library's image: (a) Lincoln Library, Springfield, Illinois, (b) Texas Trans-Pecos Library System, El Paso, (c) Northeast Texas Library System, Dallas, (d) Buda (Texas) Public Library, (e) American Library Association

Ink

Material can be printed in a number of different colored inks. Any ink other than black will cost extra; the price will range from ten dollars to twenty-five dollars for each ink change. Some copy machines now reproduce material with multicolor inks, although this service will also cost extra.

For the small library, colored ink is probably a needless expense. Unless a sophisticated copy machine is available, the material will have to be printed. It will not be possible to reproduce extra multicolored copies on most copy machines. One library staff chose stationery printed with green ink. They were forced to use a print shop to replenish the supply, as the reproduced copy was of very poor quality, and they found that letters typed with a black ribbon on green letterhead did not look professional.

Envelopes

Avoid envelopes whenever possible. Envelopes are a high-cost item, particularly if they are printed with a return address. Many flyers and invitations can be folded and stapled to form an envelope. An inexpensive stick-on label to hold the flyer together could also be used (if such can be found). The printer can score material for you, which means a line is pressed in the paper so that it will fold readily. He or she can also fold the material for you. However, there will be a charge for each score and for each fold, so this can become quite expensive. Another option is to make a line or mark on the original that can be used to indicate where the material should be folded. Volunteers or club members may be willing to do the actual folding and stapling.

Another alternative to envelopes is to use postcards. They can be purchased in sheets or created by using 65-pound weight cover paper and then cutting to size. Most copiers will easily print this weight paper. You will save both the cost of the envelope and the difference in the cost of postage.

Use of an embossing stamp or stick-on labels on envelopes can be extremely cost-effective. While you will want a supply of printed envelopes, they can be used selectively. As you choose your stationery, keep in mind that grey paper will probably need to be mailed in grey envelopes. A solution is to purchase boxes of grey envelopes and use inexpensive, preprinted, clear, peel-off labels for the return address. Incidentally, preprinted, peel-off shipping labels for use on book bags and boxes are also available.

Paper

Prices of paper vary tremendously. As you select paper, keep in mind that four factors affect cost: grade, size of the sheet, weight, and color of the sheet.

GRADE

Paper comes in a number of different grades, such as bond, coated, text, book, and cover. *Bond or offset paper* is commonly used for stationery and flyers. While paper quality used to be determined by the amount of rag content, today's bond paper rarely contains any rag content. Bond paper can vary tremendously in price. When selecting paper, ask the printer or salesperson for help. Paper can cost from one to seven cents per sheet. When the cost per sheet is multiplied by a ream of paper, the total cost quickly becomes a factor in your decision. There is no reason to purchase expensive paper for most of the work that you will be doing.

SIZE

Most paper is sold in reams of 500 sheets. You will be dealing mainly with letter size (8½ × 11 inch) or legal size (8½ × 14 inch) sheets. It will occasionally be more cost-efficient to purchase larger size paper and have it cut to your specifications. Some cover stock will be sold in reams of 250 sheets.

WEIGHT

Weight of the paper also affects the price. The true meaning of paper weight will probably remain a mystery to the layperson. Weight is currently based on the original parent size of the paper before it is cut, but it was historically determined by the size of sheepskin used for writing in the Middle Ages. In any case, concentrate on the idea that typical flyers will be printed on 20-pound paper, a flyer that you wanted to fold and mail would use 60-pound paper, and postcards or bookmarks would need 65-pound weight.

COLOR

While color affects the price of paper, the extra cost may be justified, since color is extremely important in its appeal to a potential reader. Eye catching, vivid colors will attract far more readers than white or bland shades. Light blue and pale yellow will look almost white. Very dark shades of red and blue are difficult to read. Color makes flyers stand out in a backpack full of school work or on a crowded desk. Unattractive paper is not cost effective. *Remember that the original layout sheet should be white, with the copies in color.* As you select the color for library stationery, remember that unless you have a self-correcting typewriter, colored stationery can be very difficult to correct.

Depending on your paper needs, you may want to contact a paper jobber and see if he or she will allow you to buy at wholesale prices. Be sure to send your most persuasive volunteer. Identical paper purchased at the copy shop, the office supply, a paper jobber, or a wholesaler will very tremendously in price. A seven dollar ream at the wholesaler will probably cost at least fourteen dollars at the copy shop. Like the actual cost of printing, the cost of paper is negotiable. If you live in a remote area, consider purchasing paper from a large dealer in a nearby city when someone is making a trip to town. Even basic copier paper can vary greatly in price. Remember too that it is possible to purchase your paper and then have a printer or copy shop do the actual reproductions.

Evaluation

Keep a file on publicity that you create, as well as a folder for original layouts. Indicate the number of copies, the color of paper, and the cost for each item. While the details of a publicity project may be clear to you at the time you are working on it, your memory will have collapsed by the time you need to reuse the information. Keep a scrapbook of any publicity that the library creates. You will be amazed at the quantity and the quality as time progresses. The scrapbook will also serve very effectively as a history of the library. Perhaps a board member could serve as historian and be responsible for the scrapbook.

Finally, remember to critique any work that is done. Did you choose the best layout or color of paper? Did the brochure produce any tangible results? Were you satisfied with the distribution? Evaluation can prevent future mistakes and focus attention on the positive and negative aspects of publicity. (See figure 22.)

The need to evaluate and critique all library activities is sadly underrated. Make multiple copies of the above evaluation form and keep one in a folder for each activity. You will be pleased with how useful this information is in the future.

Evaluation of _____

Market sought:

Market reached:

Number of items printed:

Paper weight:

Color used:

Layout problems:

Cost:

Comments:

Fig. 22.   Evaluation of printed materials

Conclusion

An understanding of the basic mechanics of presentation is necessary in order to create an appealing and attractive product. A well-planned publicity campaign can be sabotaged if the items used to promote the library do not have visual appeal. After years of exposure to sophisticated merchandising, people expect quality advertising. By following the suggestions presented in this chapter, you can create a product that you will be proud of that is still within the library's budget.

Recommended Reading

American Library Association. *Library Clip Art*. Chicago: ALA, 1983.
Edsall, Marian S. *Library Promotion Handbook*. Phoenix: Oryx, 1980.

Chapter 7

CREATING A MASTER PLAN

The planning process has many characteristics of housework. It is never-ending, essential, and sometimes boring. Library literature abounds with books and articles on how to analyze roles, mission statements, goals, objectives, services, and programs and how to plan for the future. Yet many libraries, particularly small ones, do not even have written policy statements. The necessity for developing a master plan cannot be overemphasized. A number of advantages result from formalizing the library's mission, goals, objectives, and policies:

The importance and role of the library will be clarified.

Decision-making is simplified with a clearly planned and established policy.

It is easier to defend decisions on the basis of accepted policy.

Written policies provide a continuity of effort from librarian to librarian.

Current allocations of existing resources are reviewed and revised on a regular basis.

Limited resources can be spent on identified priorities, rather than being diffused ineffectively.

Advantages of a master plan

The ultimate purpose of this chapter is to help the library to establish and then to *write* roles, mission statements, goals, and objectives and to evaluate the results. Libraries commit different levels of effort to the planning process. Adapt the following guidelines to fit your situation. *Remember that the purpose is to identify immediate problems and potential solutions, as well as to create a long-range plan for the library.* Much of the following material has been adapted and condensed from *Planning and Role Setting for Public Libraries.*[1] The planning process can logically be divided into the following steps.

1. Determining roles
2. Creating mission statements
3. Writing goals and objectives
4. Identifying services, activities, and programs
5. Evaluating library activities

The outline shown in figure 23 will help clarify the logical sequence of statements of intent. The meanings of various terms are described in the paragraphs that follow the outline.

SUMMARY OF ROLES, GOALS, AND OBJECTIVES

Primary Library Roles:

    Role 1:

    Role 2:

Secondary Library Roles:

    Role 3:

    Role 4:

Mission Statement: _____

_____

Goal 1:

    Objective 1.1:

    Objective 1.2:

Goal 2:

    Objective 2.1:

    Objective 2.2:

Fig. 23. An outline for writing roles, goals, and objectives. Adapted from Charles R. McClure et al., *Planning and Role Setting for Public Libraries* (Chicago: ALA, 1987), p. 55.

The Role of the Library

The first step in creating a master plan is to select one, or several, roles that best identify the philosophy of library service for your library. Libraries serve both primary and secondary roles, so you will select the primary roles that your library serves as well as the secondary roles. The typical public library *can* play eight potential roles within the community.

1. *Community activities center:* Serves as a focal point for meetings and services
2. *Community information center:* Serves as a clearinghouse for current information on other organizations, issues and services
3. *Formal education support center:* Assists students of all ages in meeting educational objectives
4. *Independent learning center:* Supports individuals of all ages who are pursuing a program of learning independent of a formal course of study
5. *Popular materials library:* Features current, high-demand materials in a variety of formats for all ages
6. *Preschoolers' door to learning:* Encourages young children to develop an interest in reading and learning through services for children and for parents and children together.
7. *Reference library:* Actively provides timely, accurate, and useful information for community residents
8. *Research center:* Assists scholars to conduct in-depth studies, investigate specific areas of knowledge, and create new knowledge.[2]

Basic to the successful organization and operation of a library is a clear statement that sets out the *mission* and philosophy of your existence. *Goals* state what you hope to accomplish, and *objectives* outline how and when the goals will be carried out. Librarians, staff, trustees, and users should be involved in the development of a mission statement, goals, and objectives. As a result, specific *policies* may then be written on topics as diverse as gift books, collection development, censorship, and circulation policies, with regular revision as growth and changes occur.

Mission Statement

Without a mission statement, how do you know what you are trying to accomplish? In recent years the term *mission statement* has appeared more frequently in the literature. If you do not already have a mission statement, it is time to write a realistic one based on the library's resources and actual funds. A mission statement enables you to establish priorities and makes known the focus of the library holdings and services. It is

DRAFTING THE MISSION STATEMENT

Most mission statements have common elements. In the space below, jot a few sentences or phrases that capture your understanding of the library's mission for the role(s) indicated and your personal perspective. Check whether the role designated is a primary or secondary role for your library.

Primary Role: _____

Role: _____   Secondary Role: _____

_____

MISSION STATEMENT ELEMENTS

Who:

_____

Needs:

_____

Supporting Services and Materials:

_____

Who: People in the community, children, young adults, seniors, families, library users, library nonusers, students, independent learners, ethnic groups, the institutionalized

Needs: Recreational, leisure, informational, educational, cultural, social, historic, civic, or intellectual needs; access to information; meeting user's needs; reaching new users; linking people with ideas; stimulating intellectual life; preserving cultural and intellectual heritage; helping individuals solve daily practical problems

Supporting Services and Materials: Fiction, nonfiction, popular materials, selected reference books, periodicals, business materials, storytime, adult education programs, juvenile materials, films, interlibrary loan, phone reference

Fig. 24.   An outline for drafting the mission statement. Adapted from Charles McClure et al., *Planning and Role Setting for Public Libraries* (Chicago: ALA, 1987), p. 44.

essential to identify the library's primary mission because the library cannot be all things to all people. Once the primary mission has been identified, available resources and effort can then be directed towards fulfilling this mission, which is the guiding force to help meet the needs and wants of the community.

Most mission statements deal with *who is affected, what needs are being addressed, and what specific library activities and materials will meet these needs.* If these three elements are incorporated into the mission statement, your work will be greatly simplified. (See figures 24 and 25.)

The _____ Public Library provides materials and services to help community residents obtain information meeting their recreational, educational, and professional needs. Special emphasis is placed on supporting students at all academic levels and on stimulating young children's interest in and appreciation for reading and learning. Fiction and nonfiction, popular materials, selected reference books, periodicals, and business materials will be the mainstay of the library holdings, but further information requests will be met through interlibrary loan cooperation and membership in the _____ Library System. The library serves as a learning and educational center for all residents of the community.

Fig. 25.   Sample mission statement

Goals

Goals are long-range statements of intent which set forth what a library strives to accomplish, who it will serve, and what resources it will use to carry out its mission. Goals should be concisely written and should relate to specific topics of major interest to the individual library. These topics will vary greatly from one library to another and may cover several areas.

Service goals:
Adult services
Children's services
Young adult services
Senior citizens
Students and cooperation with schools
Services to other special groups
Reference
Collection development
Intellectual freedom

Management goals:
   Public relations
   Facility improvement
   Staff development
   Interlibrary cooperation
   Automation for resource sharing
   Automation for public and staff use
   Finances[3]

Goals should be periodically reviewed so that consideration can be given to local and current developments, and so that the goals can be evaluated for progress and results. For example, if a local historical society opens its library to the public, it is probably a mistake for the community library to continue collecting material already available at the historical society. New library technology for the computer will probably cause you to reassess circulation procedures. The staff, whether paid or volunteer, should be aware of the library goals and take part in their formulation. As members of the community who are in constant touch with library users, staff members are attuned to library needs and interests and can be a good source for indirect community input.

Objectives

Objectives, which should be written for each goal, are revised and reviewed periodically as indicators of accomplishment. Objectives spell out a time frame for tasks to be completed and indicate what action the library will take to fulfill its goals. As with goal statements, objectives will be individualized for each library with its own particular needs and problems. In a small library, adequately serving community needs will be of primary concern, as will continually and actively involving the community in library development. As you write objectives, be certain that the objectives

   Begin with an action verb
   Are observable or measurable
   Call for only one thing to be accomplished
   Describe what is to be done
   State a specific time by which the objective is to be accomplished
   Contribute to the accomplishment of the overall goal
   Avoid use of jargon, poorly defined terms or ambiguities.[4]

Goals and related objectives may be divided into various categories, as illustrated in figure 26.

GOALS AND OBJECTIVES

The _____ Community Library is concerned with collection, organization, distribution, interpretation, and guidance in usage of its materials. Its goals fall into the general categories of building and equipment, resources, personnel, services, and finance.

A. Building and Equipment
    Goal 1: Build an attractive and accessible library facility with adequate space for its resources, staff, and users.
        Objective 1.1: Build a safe, efficient building of approximately _____ square feet by 19 ___ with accessibility for the handicapped, adequate parking, and lighting.
        Objective 1.2: Furnish the building with appropriate shelving, seating, etc.
    Goal 2: Keep abreast of new technology and apply where feasible.
        Objective 2.1: Apply for a second IBM compatible computer to further enhance services, record-keeping, and production of publicity releases.

B. Resources
    Goal 3: Provide and maintain an adequate reference collection.
        Objective 3.1: Selectively expand the reference collection.
    Goal 4: Provide and maintain a balanced collection for the information, recreation, and education interests of the community.
        Objective 4.1: Provide a balanced collection while at the same time monitoring it for current interest and needs.
        Objective 4.2: Weed materials where necessary to maximize the use of available space.
    Goal 5: Actively work with local schools and community organizations to create awareness of the library and assist students.
        Objective 5.1: Make annual presentations to all school faculty about the community library.
        Objective 5.2: Contact local organizations and make presentations whenever possible.

C. Personnel
    Goal 6: Plan for knowledgeable personnel to staff the library as envisioned by the community.
        Objective 6.1: As soon as funding allows, add a second paid staff member to relieve volunteers of undue burdens and to provide consistent knowledgeable assistance to users.
        Objective 6.2: Develop and regularly review a policy manual to cover established procedures.

D. Services
    Goal 7: Provide a friendly, welcoming atmosphere in the library.
        Objective 7.1: Educate staff and volunteers to have an open, helpful attitude at all times and to present a professional appearance to users.   (*cont.*)

Fig. 26.   Sample goals and objectives

Goal 8: Promote active community interest in library programs
and development.
Objective 8.1: Invite suggestions and criticisms from users.
Objective 8.2: Promote library resources and activities
through ongoing publicity.
Goal 9: Evaluate and review library activities.
Objective 9.1: Review and prioritize current library services
and programs.
Goal 10: Learn as much as possible about potential library users.
Objective 10.1: Gather and evaluate demographic informa-
tion about the community.

E. Finance
Goal 11: Establish and broaden a permanent funding base for
the library.
Objective 11.1: Contract by 19__ with the _____ Independent School District to provide public library service to the
residents of the area, and thus enable the library to establish a financial base for general operational expenses.
Objective 11.2: Seek private contributions to supplement
monies for expenditures for library materials.
Objective 11.3: Pursue support for funding and materials
through grant applications.

Fig. 26 (*cont.*).   Sample goals and objectives

Evaluation of Objectives

The final stage in the planning process is to evaluate the various work
done over the past year. The annual report is not sufficient. Take time to
review and analyze specific programs. Have they been worthwhile? Did
they reach the users who had been targeted? Did they accomplish a
stated objective? Do you want to repeat them? Are there alternatives to
accomplishing the same objectives? Did you have the necessary resources and staff (or volunteers) to effectively carry them out? Can the
programs be improved? A written report of results is a good indication of
how your library is fulfilling its goals and objectives. Making such a
report publicly available notifies the community and keeps people aware
of your activities and performance. It lets them know of your needs, may
help promote library use, and acts as a basis for budget requests.

Determine the effectiveness of a given activity as it pertains to each
established objective. It will be much easier to evaluate the success or
failure of an activity if you establish *in advance* the possible output
measures that can be used.

Reference services   Reference transactions per capita
Reference fill rate

Programming	Program attendance per capita
	Actual attendance
	Number of group presentations
Interlibrary loan	Number of requests
	Number of requests filled
	Percentage increase/decrease from preceding year

Programs and Services

With established objectives, the task of selecting activities is simplified. Objectives provide a framework for programs and services as well as identifying areas of specific interest. For each program, decisions must be made as to when and how it will be carried out and by whom. Refer to Chapters 2 and 5 for suggestions about format, topics, and publicity.

Policies

Written policies are necessary for informing staff and users about specific topics; policies can also be used as a point of reference when questions arise. While flexibility and judgment are inherent in the library staff's actions, written policies enhance the consistent flow of daily work, particularly in the case of a large volunteer force or in the absence of the librarian. A readily available notebook or a rotary file on the circulation desk summarizing written policies helps to clarify questions and uncertainties. There is a multitude of topics for which such policies are helpful in the small library, and each policy should be written with your own library in mind. Included in the appendixes are sample policies, forms, constitutions, and bylaws that can be readily adapted for use in your library.

Conclusion

The process of identifying and then writing specific statements about the library's roles, mission, goals, objectives, and policies is a confusing but necessary step for *all* libraries. The ability to adapt to changing conditions, to review activities, and to set new goals can be structured by formulating written criteria.

The recognition of changing conditions, and thus the ability to adapt, is greatly increased by an ongoing assessment of the library's mission and goals. Review of activities guarantees a continuing evaluation of services and programs in relationship to objectives. New goals may be identified and new objectives established. The written statements about the library are an essential ingredient of professional library management.

Notes

1. Charles R. McClure et al., *Planning and Role Setting for Public Libraries* (Chicago: American Library Association, 1987), 117.
2. Ibid., p. 28.
3. Nancy Bolt and Corinne Johnson, *Options for Small Public Libraries in Massachusetts* (Chicago: Public Library Association, 1985), 53.
4. *The Upgrade Process: Planning, Evaluating, and Measuring for Excellence in Public Library Service* (Salt Lake City: Utah State Library, 1987), 31.

Recommended Reading

Bolt, Nancy, and Corrine Johnson. *Options for Small Public Libraries in Massachusetts.* Chicago: American Library Association, 1985.
McClure, Charles R., et al. *Planning and Role Setting for Public Libraries.* Chicago: American Library Association, 1987.
Rochell, Carlton. *Wheeler and Goldhor's Practical Administration of Public Libraries.* New York: Harper and Row, 1981.
Sinclair, Dorothy M. *Administration of the Small Public Library.* 2nd ed. Chicago: American Library Association, 1979.

The end

APPENDIXES

A. Intellectual Freedom

THE LIBRARY BILL OF RIGHTS

The American Library Association affirms that all libraries are forums for information and ideas, and that the following basic policies should guide their services.

1. Books and other library resources should be provided for the interest, information, and enlightenment of all people of the community the library serves. Materials should not be excluded because of the origin, background, or views of those contributing to their creation.

2. Libraries should provide materials and information presenting all points of view on current and historical issues. Materials should not be proscribed or removed because of partisan or doctrinal disapproval.

3. Libraries should challenge censorship in the fulfillment of their responsibility to provide information and enlightenment.

4. Libraries should cooperate with all persons and groups concerned with resisting abridgment of free expression and free access to ideas.

5. A person's right to use a library should not be denied or abridged because of origin, age, background, or views.

6. Libraries which make exhibit spaces and meeting rooms available to the public they serve should make such facilities available on an equitable basis, regardless of the beliefs or affiliations of individuals or groups requesting their use.

Adopted by the American Library Association Council, June 18, 1948. Amended February 2, 1961, June 27, 1967, and January 23, 1980.

FREEDOM TO READ

1. It is in the public interest for publishers and librarians to make available the widest diversity of views and expressions, including those which are unorthodox or unpopular with the majority.

    Creative thought is by definition new, and what is new is different. The bearer of every new thought is a rebel until his idea is refined and tested. Totalitarian systems attempt to maintain themselves in power by the ruthless suppression of any concept which challenges the established orthodoxy. The power of a democratic system to adapt to change is vastly strengthened by the freedom of its citizens to choose widely from among conflicting opinions offered freely to them. To stifle every nonconformist idea at birth would mark the end of the democratic process. Furthermore, only through the constant activity of weighing and selecting can the democratic mind attain the strength demanded by times like these. We need to know not only what we believe but why we believe it.

2. Publishers, librarians, and booksellers do not need to endorse every idea or presentation contained in the books they make available. It would conflict with the public interest for them to establish their own political, moral, or aesthetic views as a standard for determining what books should be published or circulated.

    Publishers and librarians serve the educational process by helping to make available knowledge and ideas required for the growth of the mind and the increase of learning. They do not foster education by imposing as mentors the patterns of their own thought. The people should have the freedom to read and consider a broader range of ideas than those that may be held by any single librarian or publisher or government or church. It is wrong that what one man can read should be confined to what another thinks proper.

3. It is contrary to the public interest for publishers or librarians to determine the acceptability of a book on the basis of the personal history or political affiliations of the author.

    A book should be judged as a book. No art or literature can flourish if it is to be measured by the political views or private lives of its creators. No society of free men can flourish which draws up lists of writers to whom it will not listen, whatever they may have to say.

4. There is no place in our society for efforts to coerce the taste of others, to confine adults to the reading matter deemed suitable for adolescents, or to inhibit the efforts of writers to achieve artistic expression.

    To some, much of modern literature is shocking. But is not much of life itself shocking? We cut off literature at the source if we prevent writers from dealing with the stuff of life. Parents and teachers have a responsibility to prepare the young to meet the diversity of experiences in life to which they will be exposed, as they have a responsibility to help them

A joint statement by the American Library Association and the Association of American Publishers, originally issued in 1953. *Books* as used in this statement includes all kinds of materials acquired for library use.

learn to think critically for themselves. These are affirmative responsibilities, not to be discharged simply by preventing them from reading works for which they are not yet prepared. In these matters taste differs, and taste cannot be legislated; nor can machinery be devised which will suit the demands of one group without limiting the freedom of others.

5. It is not in the public interest to force a reader to accept with any book the prejudgment of a label characterizing the book or author as subversive or dangerous.

    The idea of labeling presupposes the existence of individuals or groups with wisdom to determine by authority what is good or bad for the citizen. It presupposes that each individual must be directed in making up his mind about the ideas he examines. But Americans do not need others to do their thinking for them.

6. It is the responsibility of publishers and librarians, as guardians of the people's freedom to read, to contest encroachments upon that freedom by individuals or groups seeking to impose their own standards or tastes upon the community at large.

    It is inevitable in the give and take of the democratic process that the political, the moral, or the aesthetic concepts of an individual or group will occasionally collide with those of another individual or group. In a free society each individual is free to determine for himself what he wishes to read, and each group is free to determine what it will recommend to its freely associated members. But no group has the right to take the law into its own hands, and to impose its own concept of politics or morality upon other members of a democratic society. Freedom is no freedom if it is accorded only to the accepted and the inoffensive.

7. It is the responsibility of publishers and librarians to give full meaning to the freedom to read by providing books that enrich the quality and diversity of thought and expression. By the exercise of this affirmative responsibility, bookmen can demonstrate that the answer to a bad book is a good one, the answer to a bad idea is a good one.

    The freedom to read is of little consequence when expended on the trivial; it is frustrated when the reader cannot obtain matter fit for his purpose. What is needed is not only the absence of restraint, but the positive provision of opportunity for the people to read the best that has been thought and said. Books are the major channel by which the intellectual inheritance is handed down, and the principal means of its testing and growth. The defense of their freedom and integrity, and the enlargement of their service to society, requires of all bookmen the utmost of their faculties, and deserves of all citizens the fullest of their support.

    We state these propositions neither lightly nor as easy generalizations. We here stake out a lofty claim for the value of books. We do so because we believe that they are good, possessed of enormous variety and usefulness, worthy of cherishing and keeping free. We realize that the application of these propositions may mean the dissemination of ideas and manners of expression that are repugnant to many persons. We do not state these propositions in the comfortable belief that what people read is unimportant. We believe rather that what people read is deeply important; that ideas can be dangerous; but that the suppression of ideas is fatal to a democratic society. Freedom itself is a dangerous way of life, but it is ours.

FREEDOM TO VIEW

The freedom to view, along with the freedom to speak, to hear, and to read, is protected by the First Amendment to the Constitution of the United States. In a free society, there is no place for censorship of any medium of expression. Therefore, we affirm these principles:

1. It is in the public interest to provide the broadest possible access to films and other audiovisual materials because they have proven to be among the most effective means for the communication of ideas. Liberty of circulation is essential to insure the constitutional guarantee of freedom of expression.

2. It is in the public interest to provide for our audiences films and other audiovisual materials which represent a diversity of views and expression. Selection of a work does not constitute or imply agreement with or approval of the content.

3. It is our professional responsibility to resist the constraint of labeling or prejudging a film on the basis of the moral, religious, or political beliefs of the producer or film maker or on the basis of controversial content.

4. It is our professional responsibility to contest vigorously, by all lawful means, every encroachment upon the public's freedom to view.

Drafted by the Educational Film Library Association Freedom to View Committee and adopted by the EFLA Board in February 1979.

B. Policies

SAMPLE BOOK SELECTION POLICY

It is the function of the _____ Community Library to provide materials for all ages, from preschool through maturity. The aim of the adult book collection is to make available books and other materials that will meet educational, informational, cultural, and recreational interests and needs of the patrons. To fulfill this purpose, the library endeavors to maintain a carefully selected collection of good, representative books of permanent value and of current interest. Each title is judged individually according to its intrinsic merit, the subject treated, the reader interest, and the need for the book in an organized collection. Each title is judged as a whole, and isolated passages in themselves are not used as criteria.

The children's collection is selected to provide pleasurable reading for reading's sake and, insofar as possible, to provide information in all fields of knowledge which are of interest to children. The collection is carefully selected for children of all ages and abilities, and emphasis is placed upon books which stimulate imagination, mental growth, and the development of taste for good literature and beautifully made books.

Young people's books are selected with the aim of helping teenagers find self-realization, live useful, well-adjusted lives in the community, and know and understand the world at large. The books are selected to widen the adolescent's thinking, to enrich his life, and to help him fulfill his recreational and emotional needs.

The library will provide, as far as possible, materials treating all sides of controversial issues—materials that give evidence of a sincere desire to be factual, that are written in a reasonable fashion, and that show results of careful study.

Materials on controversial issues that present only one side of a question and are written in a violent, sensational, and inflammatory manner will ordinarily not be selected. Books of doubtful value, such as campaign biographies or fiction about which there is great curiosity, will occasionally be acquired by the library; these kinds of materials will be discarded when they have served their purpose of meeting a strong, though temporary, demand.

Since it is possible to make a mistake in applying these principles, the librarian stands ready to review individual decisions upon written request. [See Request for Reconsideration form, Appendix D.] Such requests will be considered by the librarian and/or the board of directors.

SAMPLE CIRCULATION POLICY

All books, periodicals, and tapes may be checked out for a two-week period, with renewal privileges available unless there is a waiting list.

Reference books and current periodicals are for in-library use only.

Fines are charged for overdue books at the following rates: $.05 per day for children's books and $.10 per day for adult titles. No fines will be charged for days that the library is closed.

Replacements for lost borrower cards will be $.25.

Charges for lost or damaged books are based on replacement cost plus a $2.50 per item processing charge.

The library will be open the following hours:
Monday through Thursday   10–6
Friday   10–4
Saturday   10–1
The library will be closed on the following holidays:
Thanksgiving Day
Christmas Day
New Year's Day
Memorial Day
July 4th

POLICY ON CONFIDENTIALITY OF LIBRARY RECORDS*

The Council of the American Library Association strongly recommends that the responsible officers of each library, cooperative system, and consortium in the United States:

*Note: See also ALA POLICY MANUAL 54.15—CODE OF ETHICS, point #3, "Librarians must protect each user's right to privacy with respect to information sought or received, and materials consulted, borrowed, or acquired."

1. Formally adopt a policy which specifically recognizes its circulation records and other records identifying the names of library users to be confidential in nature.

2. Advise all librarians and library employees that such records shall not be made available to any agency of state, federal, or local government except pursuant to such process, order, or subpoena as may be authorized under the authority of, and pursuant to, federal, state, or local law relating to civil, criminal, or administrative discovery procedures or legislative investigative power.

3. Resist the issuance or enforcement of any such process, order, or subpoena until such time as a proper showing of good cause has been made in a court of competent jurisdiction.**

    **Note: Point 3, above, means that upon receipt of such process, order, or subpoena, the library's officers will consult with their legal counsel to determine if such process, order, or subpoena is in proper form and if there is a showing of good cause for its issuance; if the process, order, or subpoena is not in proper form or if good cause has not been shown, they will insist that such defects be cured.

    Adopted January 20, 1971; revised July 4, 1975, July 2, 1986, by the ALA Council.

GIFTS

Sample Policy I

The library accepts gifts of books, pamphlets, periodicals, films, phonograph records, and the like with the understanding that they will be added to the collection only when needed. The library makes an effort to dispose carefully and thoughtfully of all gift material which it does not add to its own collection.

The following receipt will be used, except in cases of donations of items of exceptional value.

The _____ Library wishes to acknowledge the donation of the following:
(list number of books, not actual titles)

Received by: _____

Date: _____

Donated by: _____

The dollar value of these donated materials will be determined by the donor. The library would like to thank you for your tax deductible contribution. Your continued support is greatly appreciated.

_____, Librarian

Sample Policy 2

The library receives many gifts of books, periodicals, and other materials, for which we are always grateful. In order to avoid misunderstanding about the disposition of gifts, however, it is suggested that prospective donors read the following statement:

The library adheres to a carefully planned policy in accepting gifts. It reserves the right to decide whether or not the gift is to be added to the library collection. The book may be: (1) a duplicate of an item of which no more copies are needed; (2) outdated; (3) of no reference or circulation value; (4) in poor condition, such that the cost of repair could not be justified.

Useful but unneeded gifts are sold, with the receipts added to the acquisition funds. Those not so used are disposed of.

The library regrets that it cannot appraise gifts. As recipients, our evaluations would be questioned by tax officials. On request, however, we will be glad to provide a statement describing the gift.

Edwin Castagna, "Collections," in *Local Public Library Administration*, 2nd ed. (Chicago: American Library Association, 1980) 150.

SAMPLE DISPLAYS AND EXHIBITS POLICY

Exhibitions and displays of books, realia, and objects of art shall be part of the library's program for encouraging appreciation and understanding of the subject of the exhibit. Such exhibitions and displays are subject to the limitations of space, facilities, and staff time.

The library will try to protect materials displayed, but it cannot be responsible for loss or damage to such materials.

C. Constitution and Bylaws

SAMPLE COMMUNITY LIBRARY BYLAWS

Article I

The name of this organization shall be the _____ Community Library, Incorporated.

Article II

Purpose

The purpose of this corporation is to provide library facilities and services for residents of the _____ Independent School District. This corporation is formed exclusively for educational purposes as described in Section 501(c)(3) of the Internal Revenue Code.

Article III

Membership

Section I. Membership shall be composed of those persons residing in the _____ Independent School District who hold valid library cards.

Section II. Voting members must be eighteen years of age or older.

Article IV

Board of Directors and Officers

Section I. The elective officers of this board shall be president, vice-president, secretary, treasurer, and corresponding secretary. These officers shall comprise the executive board of the corporation.

Section II. Officers of the board shall be elected at the annual meeting of the membership at large and shall assume office at the first meeting of the calendar year. Officers shall serve for terms of one year. No officer shall be eligible for election to the same office for more than two consecutive years. Any vacancy occurring in any office shall be filled by the board of directors from the existing membership. The replacement officer shall complete the unexpired term.

Section III. A nominating committee shall be appointed annually by the board president and shall be composed of a chairman and two other members, one of whom shall be a member of the board of directors. This committee shall be responsible for recommending a single slate of officers for the executive committee, as well as recommending directors to the board to fill expired terms or increase membership as needed. Additional nominations may be made from the floor provided the consent of the nominee shall first have been obtained. If there is more than one candidate for the same office, election shall be by ballot, and a majority vote shall elect.

Section IV. Resignations from the board shall be made in writing. Any vacancies on the board shall be filled by the board, and such appointment shall be for the length of the term vacated.

Section V. In addition, the board may provide for ex-officio members and appoint committees as they deem advisable.

Article V

Duties of the Officers

The officers shall have the usual duties and authority exercised by officers of a nonprofit corporation.

Article VI

Meetings and Quorum

Section I. The regular meetings of the board shall be at a time and place designated by the board. Six members shall constitute a quorum.

Section II. Special meetings of the board may be called by the president or upon the request of any three members of the board.

Section III. Attendance at board meetings shall be mandatory. Legitimate absences from meetings shall require notification in advance of the meeting. If any board member has two consecutive unexcused absences, that member will be notified in writing. If a third consecutive unexcused absence occurs, the member will automatically be removed from the board.

Section IV. A meeting of the membership at large may be called at any time by the board; however, an annual meeting shall be called prior to the beginning of the next calendar year at which time an executive committee and new members to the board shall be elected. Notice of such meetings shall be posted in the library and, when feasible, printed in the local newspaper at least one week prior to the meeting. A majority of the members present and voting at the meeting constitute a quorum.

Article VII

Policy

Section I. All rules, regulations, and policies governing the library shall be set by the board.

Section II. The librarian shall be selected by the board.

Article VIII

Amendments

The board of directors shall adopt and amend the bylaws. Bylaws may be amended by majority vote of the directors present at any meeting of the board, a quorum being present. Proposed changes shall have been submitted in writing to each director at least two weeks prior to the meeting at which action is taken.

Article IX

Parliamentary Procedure

Robert's Rules of Order, Newly Revised, when not in conflict with these bylaws, shall govern the proceedings of the board.

SAMPLE FRIENDS OF THE LIBRARY CONSTITUTION

Article I

Name

The name of the organization shall be the Friends of the _____ Library.

Article II

Purpose

Section I. The Friends of the _____ Library shall be a nonpolicymaking and nonprofit organization, the object of which shall be to promote the interest and welfare of the _____ Library as a cultural and educational asset to the citizens residing within the boundaries of the ———— Independent School District and to support the policies established by the library board of trustees.

Section II. Funds shall be expended in accordance with the purpose of the organization and on approval of the executive board of the Friends.

Section III. In the event that this organization should for any reason be dissolved, all monies shall be given to the ———— Library.

Article III

Members

Anyone interested in the Friends of the ———— Library may become a member by paying the dues specified in the bylaws. Membership shall be renewable annually.

Article IV

Officers and Elections

Section I. The officers of the organization shall consist of a president, a vice-president, a secretary, and a treasurer, all of whom shall be drawn from the members of the organization.

Section II. Nominations for office shall be made by a committee appointed by the executive board. Additional nominations may be made from the floor at the time of election provided that the consent of the person nominated has been obtained before the nomination is made.

Article V

Executive Board

Section I. The officers and chairpersons of standing committees shall constitute the executive board, of which the president and secretary shall be chairman and secretary, respectively.

Section II. The executive board shall manage all affairs of the organization.

Section III. The chairman of the library board of trustees and the librarian of the ———— Library shall be ex-officio members of the executive board.

Section IV. Meetings of the executive board shall be held at the call of the chairperson or upon the written request of three members of the executive board, due notice having been given.

Section V. The executive board shall fill vacancies in executive offices for the unexpired term. (When expedient, the chairperson may assume this duty.)

Article VI

Committees

Section I. Standing committees shall be library services, used book store, program, children's activities, membership, publicity, and hospitality.

Section II. Special committees may be appointed as required.

Article VII

Quorum

Section I. A quorum at the annual meeting shall consist of members present, provided two officers are present.

Section II. Two officers and a majority of the standing committee chairpersons shall constitute a quorum of the executive board.

Article VIII

Parliamentary Authority

Parliamentary authority shall be *Robert's Rules of Order, Newly Revised,* provided it is consistent with the organization's constitution and bylaws.

Article IX

Amendments

These bylaws may be amended at any meeting of the organization by a two-thirds majority of the members present and voting, provided that a written copy of the proposed amendment, signed by two members, has been submitted to the executive board and, in turn, posted by the secretary in the _____ Library at least fifteen days prior to the meeting.

SAMPLE FRIENDS OF THE LIBRARY BYLAWS

Article I

Membership and Dues

Section I. Types of membership shall be:
    Individual membership: $10.00
    Family membership: $25.00
    Patron: $50.00
    Sponsor: $100.00
    Corporate membership: $250.00
    Life membership: $1,000.00 or more

Section II. Annual membership dues shall be renewable in April of each year.

Article II

Officers

Section I. The officers of the organization shall consist of a president, a vice-president, a secretary, and a treasurer.

Section II. Outgoing officers shall deliver to their successors in office all records and other materials belonging to their office at the close of the term.

Article III

Duties of Officers

Section I. The president shall preside at all meetings, approve all bills for payment, appoint all committees after consulting with the other officers, and report to the _____ Library Board of Trustees on a regular basis.

Section II. The vice-president shall act as parliamentarian at meetings and, in the absence of the president, shall perform the duties of that office.

Section III. The secretary shall be responsible for the correct recording of the minutes of meetings and shall present the minutes of previous meetings and assist with correspondence.

Section IV. The treasurer shall be the custodian of the funds, which shall be deposited to the account of the Friends of the _____ Library in a bank designated by the executive board. He or she shall also keep accurate and complete records of the funds and be prepared to report on them at each executive board meeting, the annual meeting, or at the request of the president.

Article IV

Terms of Office

Section I. Terms of office shall begin immediately upon election.

Section II. Officers shall be elected to serve one-year terms.

D. Sample Forms

REQUEST FOR RECONSIDERATION OF A BOOK OR OTHER LIBRARY MATERIAL

To the person requesting reconsideration: Library policy requires that complaints be made on this form for discussion in detail. The materials selection policy will be made available to you. Thank you for taking the time to provide information.

Author _____

Title _____

Publisher or Producer _____

Request initiated by _____

Telephone _____ Address _____

City _____ Zip Code _____

Requester represents: individual   _____

organization   _____

other group   _____

Check one: _____ Book _____ Paperback _____ Magazine _____ Film

_____ Pamphlet _____ Picture _____ Other _____

Specifically, to what do you object? (Cite pages, instances, etc.) _____

_____

What do you feel might be the result of reading, hearing, or seeing this material?

_____

_____

Is there anything good about this material? _____

_____

Did you read the entire book or examine the entire item? _____

What parts? _____

Are you aware of the judgment of this material by professional critics? _____

_____

What do you believe is the theme of this book or material? _____

_____

What would you like to have your library do about this material? _____

_____

_____   _____

Date   Signature of complainant

INTERLIBRARY LOAN REQUEST

Date _____   Needed by _____

Author: (or periodical)
Last Name _____   First Name _____

Title _____

_____

Publisher _____   Date _____

Call Number _____

Patron's Name _____

Home Telephone _____   Work Telephone _____

Postage: $1.00 per book—payable in advance _____

Subject Request _____

_____

Material already used or not appropriate: _____

_____

Person taking request: _____

Verified in   BIP _____   Other _____

Dates: Received _____   Due _____   Returned _____

BIBLIOGRAPHY

ALA Yearbook of Library and Information Services, 1985. Chicago: American Library Association, 1985.

ALA Yearbook of Library and Information Services, 1986. Chicago: American Library Association, 1986.

Alvarez, Robert S. "From the Editor's Desk." *Library Administrator's Digest* 22 (April 1987):29–30.

———. "Impact! Community Awareness Project." *Library Administrator's Digest* 20 (May 1985): 72.

American Library Association. *Library Clip Art*. Chicago: ALA, 1983.

Baeckler, Virginia, and Linda Larson. *GO, PEP, and POP!* New York: The Unabashed Librarian, 1976.

Ballard, Thomas H. "Library Buildings: Form Follows Function?" *Library Journal* 110 (December 1985):44–46.

Beach, Cecil. "Local Funding of Public Libraries." *Library Journal* 110 (June 15, 1985):27–28.

Bessant, Donna I. "What a School Librarian Would Like to Say to a Public Librarian about Young Adult Services." *Illinois Libraries* 65 (September 1983):449–51.

Bolt, Nancy, and Corrine Johnson. *Options for Small Public Libraries in Massachusetts*. Chicago: Public Library Association, 1985.

Bonnell, Pamela G. *Fund Raising for the Small Library*. Chicago: American Library Association, 1983.

Brandehoff, Susan E. "The 'ideal' public library—videocassettes a top priority." *American Libraries* 17 (December 1986):859.

———. "Opinion Survey Shows Untaxed Areas Would Say 'Yes' to Library Levies." *American Libraries* 17 (December 1986):859.

Bronson, Que. *Books on Display*. Washington, D.C.: Metropolitan Washington Library Council, 1982.

Cavanagh, J. Albert. *Lettering and Alphabets*. New York: Dover, 1946.

Dubberly, Ronald A. "Why You Must Know Your Library's Mission." *Public Libraries* 22 (Fall 1983):89–90.

Edsall, Marian S. *Library Promotion Handbook*. Phoenix: Oryx, 1980.

Fish, Jim. "Community Analysis." *Bay State Librarian* 67 (June 1978):17–19.

Freiser, Leonard H. "Fundraising and the Meaning of Public Support." *Library Journal* 110 (June 15, 1985):29–31.

Gaines, Bob. "Collection Management Notes." *Central Texas Library System Newsletter* (March 1987):1–3.

Gaughan, Karen. "Working with Organizations." *The Unabashed Librarian* 51 (January 1984):5–7.

Goldhor, Herbert. "Community Analysis for the Public Library." *Illinois Libraries* 62 (April 1980):296–302.

Haight, Anne Lyon. *Banned Books 387 B.C. to 1978 A.D.* Updated and enlarged by Chandler B. Grannis. New York: Bowker, 1978.

Hamburg, Morris, et al. *Library Planning and Decision-making Systems.* Cambridge, Mass.: MIT Press, 1974.

Head, John W. "The National Rural Library Reference Service." *RQ* 23 (Spring 1984):316–21.

Hennen, Thomas J., Jr. "Attacking the Myths of Small Libraries." *American Libraries* 16 (December 1986):830–84.

Hildebrand, Susan. "Texas at Bottom in Literacy." *Library Developments* 8 (August 1986):4.

Howard, Edward N. *Local Power and the Community Library.* Chicago: American Library Association, 1978.

Ihrig, Alice B. *Texas Public Library Trustee Manual.* Austin: Texas State Library, 1982.

Johnson, Debra Wilcox. *Libraries and Literacy.* Chicago: American Library Association, 1987.

Kadanoff, Diane Gordon. "Small Libraries—No Small Job!" *Library Journal* 111 (March 1, 1986):72–73.

———. "Small Library Options." *Library Journal* 111 (September 1, 1986):164–65.

Lareau, Bill. "How to Spot a Potential Leader." *Personal Report for the Executive* (September 17, 1985):1–2.

Lathshaw, Patricia H. "Evaluating Your Public Relations Program." *ALA Bulletin* 48 (April 1978):32–34.

Leamon, David L. "No Fees for Services." *Library Administrator's Digest* 12 (June 1987):46.

Leisner, Tony. "Mission Statements and the Marketing Mix." *Public Libraries* 25 (Fall 1986):86–87.

Liebold, Louise Condak. *Fireworks, Brass Bands and Elephants.* Phoenix: Oryx, 1987.

Local Public Library Administration. 2nd ed. Ellen Altman, ed. Chicago: American Library Association, 1980.

Manley, Will. "Facing the Public." *Wilson Library Bulletin* 58 (June 1984):730–31.

Martin, Allie Beth. "Studying the Community." *Library Trends* 24 (January 1976):433–40.

McClure, Charles R., et al. *Planning and Role Setting for Public Libraries.* Chicago: American Library Association, 1987.

Palmour, Vernon E., Marcia C. Bellassai, and Nancy V. DeWath. *A Planning Process for Public Libraries.* Chicago: American Library Association, 1980.

Pollet, Dorothy, and Peter C. Kaskell, eds. *Sign Systems for Libraries.* New York: Bowker, 1979.

PR Primer. Chicago: ALA Public Information Office, 1987.

Razzano, Barbara Will. "Creating the Library Habit." *Library Journal* 110 (February 15, 1985):111–14.

Rochell, Carlton. *Wheeler and Goldhor's Practical Administration of Public Libraries*. Rev. ed. New York: Harper and Row, 1981.

Rossie, Charles M., Jr. *Media Resource Guide: How to Tell Your Story*. 4th ed. Los Angeles: Foundation for American Communications, 1985.

Saunders, John A. "Mission Imperceptible." *Library Association Record* 88 (March 1986):126–27.

Scheppke, James B. "Management." *Texas Library Journal* 60 (Spring 1984):18–19.

Setterberg, Fred, and Kary Schulman. *Beyond Profit: The Complete Guide to Managing the Nonprofit Organization*. New York: Harper and Row, 1985.

Sinclair, Dorothy M. *Administration of the Small Public Library*. 2nd ed. Chicago: American Library Association, 1979.

Starry, Michael. "Effective Library Promotion Builds Better Financial Support." *PNLA Quarterly* 38 (Summer 1974):17–19.

Thorne, Judy. "Behavior: Putting the Power of Color to Work," *Extra* (April 1981):34–39.

The Upgrade Process: Planning, Evaluating, and Measuring for Excellence in Public Library Service. Salt Lake City: Utah State Library, 1987.

Van House, Nancy A. "Public Library Effectiveness." *Library Information Science Research* 8 (July 1986):261–83.

Wheeler, Joseph L., and Herbert Goldhor. *Practical Administration of Public Libraries*. New York: Harper and Row, 1962.

Young, Virginia, ed. *The Library Trustee: A Practical Guidebook*. 4th ed. Chicago: American Library Association, 1988.

Zweizig, Douglas. "Community Analysis." In *Local Public Library Administration*. 2nd ed. Ellen Altman, ed. Chicago: American Library Association, 1980.

INDEX

Services 27–29, 31–36, 37–39, 67–69, 115
    checklist of 36–40
    evaluation of 36, 40
Signage 64–65, 91, 96–99
    appearance checklist 70–72
State legislative libraries 19
State library systems 18–19
    workshops 11
Stationery 101–105
Statistics 27, 114–115
    see also Census; Circulation, statistics;
        Community statistics
Storytime *see* Programs, storytime
Summer reading program *see* Programs,
        summer reading

Tapes 32–33
Television 80–82
    controversial material in interview 81–
        82
    public service announcement 80–81
    topics 79–80
Tucson Public Library 32
Typesets *see* Printing

Users, library 5, 25–26, 31–32, 36, 75, 77
    attitude toward 67–69, 72–73
    community needs 23–26
    registration 69
    student 14–15, 73, 83–84, 85

Vertical files 34–35
Victoria Public Library 14, 84
Videocassettes 32–33
Volunteers 1–10, 48–56, 85, 89
    at home 7–8
    appreciation of 5, 7, 8, 10, 89
    groups 3, 6–7, 8, 52, 65
    problems with 3–4
    recruitment of 2–3, 5–7, 9, 14, 90
    responsibilities of 4, 67–69
    socializing among 2–3, 5
    teenagers 2, 8–10, 52
    training 3–4, 7–10
    work assignments of 2–4
    see also Friends of the library

Weeding 33–34, 66
Westbank Community Library 1–2, 5, 16,
    53, 54, 83, 91, 95

Beth Wheeler Fox is director of the Westbank Community Library in Austin, Texas. She has worked as a reference librarian in the Palos Verdes (California) Public Library and as branch librarian of the Fort Benning (Georgia) Base Library. In 1986, the Westbank Community Library won a John Cotton Dana Library Public Relations Special Award for exceptional public relations work.